R.E.I. Editions

All our ebooks can be read on the following devices:

- Computer
- eReader
- iOS
- Android
- Blackberry
- Window
- Tablet
- Mobile phone

Cloaks - Brown - Kittel - Graf

Her Majesty the Spitfire

ISBN: 9782372975315

Publication: December 2024

www.rei-editions.com

Mantelli - Brown - Kittel - Graf

Her Majesty The Spitfire

REI Editions

Index

Supermarine Spitfire

Her Majesty the Spitfire.

This aircraft is an air legend, a true brand, and its image is inextricably linked to the British victory in the Battle of Britain.

- It is one of the very few aircraft, perhaps the only one, whose name evokes some images even in a layman of historical aviation things.

The Supermarine Spitfire is probably the most famous aircraft of the Second World War.
By the time production ended, over 20,000 Spitfires had been built, and the aircraft had changed engines, its loaded weight had doubled and its top speed had increased by 90 miles per hour.

- Despite these changes, the 1945 Spitfire is immediately recognisable as part of the same family as the 1936 prototype.

However, it was also an aircraft that, at a certain point, had its day: despite being an excellent defensive machine, heavily armed, very agile and very fast in climbing, the lack of range and sufficient load capacity did not help it in the continuation of the war.
In fact, when the Allied missions became increasingly offensive and long-range, while the Bf-109, not very suitable for escort actions, remained valid because from an offensive fighter, albeit short-range, it moved to the more suitable short-range interception roles, over the skies of the mother country increasingly attacked by Flying Fortresses, the Spitfire remained on the sidelines and recovered some merit when it was able to have advanced air bases on the continent.
His victory against his arch-enemy Bf-109 was however a worthy end to his war career, at least considering the Second World War: from the first Bf-109Es against the Spitfire Mk I to the last Bf-109Ks against the Spitfire Mk XIV, thousands and

thousands of air combats have left a vast literature and numerous memories on the part of the pilots, often becoming aces of the calibre of Jonnie Johnson or Adolph Galland.
The Supermarine Spitfire was a single-seat, single-engine, low-wing fighter aircraft (the wing was positioned below the fuselage, with the centre of gravity located above the point of application of lift, making the aircraft more unstable but at the same time giving it greater manoeuvrability) produced by the British Supermarine Aviation Works in the 1930s and 1940s.
In the Battle of Britain, it shared with the Hurricane the difficult task of defending the capital from Luftwaffe attacks.
Used by the air forces of numerous Allied countries such as the Soviet Union, Australia and the United States of America, it was the only Allied fighter produced for the entire duration of the war.

- The Spitfire is not a single aircraft with various modifications and improvements, but a real family of aircraft that has covered all roles and adapted to no less than 10 years of technological evolution, from the first Spitfires with their 1,000 hp Merlin engines and two-bladed propellers, to the latest with the Griffons of over 2,000 hp and 5-bladed metal propellers or even two counter-rotating three-bladed ones.

Propellers and engines alone weighed about the same as the Spitfire Mk.I.
It was built in about forty versions, a quantity greater than that of any other British aircraft.

- Including the 2,556 Seafires, 20,351 were produced until 1947, when the last Mk.24 rolled off the assembly lines.

After the war it was used for a long time by the air forces of France, Holland, Greece, Turkey, Belgium, India, Italy and Czechoslovakia.
The RAF's last front-line operational mission was flown on 1 April 1954 by a PR19 Spitfire reconnaissance aircraft of No. 81 Squadron RAF.

But the Spitfire continued to be used for another three years by the Temperature and Humidity Flight, for meteorological measurements, until June 1957, when it was decommissioned.

- It was considered by British ace Johnnie Johnson to be "the finest conventional defensive fighter of the war".

History

The Spitfire was the masterpiece of Reginald Joseph Mitchell, already known as a designer of seaplanes for the Schneider Cup, won in 1927 by one of his aircraft: the Supermarine S.5.
Two of his other designs, the S.6 and the S6.B, had won again in 1929 and 1931.
The S.6B also raised the world speed record to 655 km/h.
In 1934, Mitchell submitted the Supermarine Type 224 to the Royal Air Force for a competition to select a new fighter type. But the aircraft proved to be a failure.
Its top speed was only 367 km/h, and it took 9 minutes and 30 seconds to reach 4,575 meters, while the cooling system was defective.
The competition was won by the Gloster Gladiator, but Mitchell did not give up.
When the Air Ministry, again in 1934, issued Specification F 5/34, which called for an aircraft with a covered cockpit, retractable undercarriage and an armament of 8 machine guns, Mitchell proposed the Supermarine Type 300, the future Spitfire.
The Type 300, according to Mitchell's original idea, was, in essence, the smallest and simplest fighter aircraft that could be built around the Rolls-Royce PV-12 engine.
Two clear winners emerged: the F.36/34, later to become the Hurricane, and the F.37/34, which was the Type 300, later christened the Spitfire.
Approval from the Air Ministry for the construction of the F.37/34 prototype arrived in January 1935.

- It had a linear structure, a light alloy half-shell fuselage, and a single-spar wing, covered in metal, except for the ailerons covered in painted canvas, retractable landing gear and machine guns housed in the wing that fired out from the propeller disk.

As the Air Ministry had decided that future fighters should have eight machine guns, Mitchell designed the wing of the Type 300

to be markedly elliptical, so that the eight machine guns could all be located as far away from the fuselage as possible and the ammunition tanks could be quickly refilled through hatches in the skin.
This feature turned out to be one of the best designed for a fighter of the time.
Among the features of the Supermarine Spitfire, which had a water-glycol liquid-cooled engine, is a strange asymmetrical placement of the radiators: under the left wing the cooling radiator and under the right wing the oil radiator.

- Ethylene glycol, instead of water, which has a higher boiling point (around 193°), allowed operating at higher temperatures, thus improving the radiator's efficiency (the higher the temperature of the liquid, the greater the quantity of heat released to the air under the same conditions) and therefore allowing a reduction in its surface area of around 50%.

Other distinctive features include slotted wing flaps, a comfortable cockpit covered by a sliding Perpex (clear acrylic plastic) canopy, six side exhaust pipes, a fixed tail skid and a heavy two-bladed wooden propeller.
This first aircraft (K50549) first flew on 5 March 1936 from Eastleigh Airport, better known today as Southampton Airport, powered, as specified, by a Merlin "C" engine, Rolls-Royce engine designation PV-12, of 900 hp (671 kW).
The pilot who flew it was Captain Joseph "Mutt" Summers, Vickers' chief test pilot, who had the propeller and engine replaced during the first four flights.

- The Spitfire was rated very good but not perfect.

The rudder was too sensitive and the top speed was disappointing: 531 km/h, slower than the Hurricane she had flown five months earlier. With a new wooden propeller she reached 560 km/h.
In the meantime the Air Ministry had drawn up a second specification, F.16/36, relating to the production and development of fighters.

On 3 June 1936, less than two months after the prototype's first flight , Supermarine received an order for 310 Spitfire Is, expanded the following year by a further 200 aircraft.

- Each Spitfire cost around £9,500.

The most expensive components were the fuselage, hand-crafted and finished, costing £2,500, then the Rolls-Royce Merlin engine, at £2,000, followed by the wings at £1,800 a pair, machine guns and landing gear, both at £800 each, and the propeller, at £350.

The Air Ministry suggested a number of names for the new aircraft built at the Vickers-Armstrongs works, all with the same initial of the manufacturer, S for Supermarine. Several alternatives were proposed, including Shrew and Shrike.

The name Spitfire was suggested by Sir Robert MacLean, the director of Vickers-Armstrongs at the time, who called his daughter Ann "a little spitfire", an Elizabethan expression for a fiery person.

The name was previously also used to designate the Type 224.

Meanwhile, between 1937 and 1938, the prototype K5054 was subjected to continuous tests.

- The wings also housed armament consisting of eight 7.7 mm machine guns, arranged outside the propeller disc.

England, unlike several other European nations and the United States, which preferred to orient themselves towards heavier weapons, 12.7 or 20 mm, chose, in order to obtain the high firepower necessary for modern fighter aircraft, intended to fight at speeds of the order of 500 km/h or more, batteries of numerous light weapons, characterised by a high rate of fire: however, since these had to be installed in the wings, out of reach of the pilot, and since the Vickers machine gun, the traditional weapon of English fighters, did not guarantee sufficient reliability, it was necessary to resort to the licensed production of a new machine gun.

After a comparison with various weapons of the established calibre, the American Colt Browning was chosen, which was produced under licence by BSA (Birmingham Small Arms) Guns Ltd.

- After the installation of machine guns, it was noted that they tended to jam when reaching high altitudes, due to the low air temperature and the formation of ice, which blocked the firing mechanisms.

To overcome this problem, a long and complicated system was developed to send hot air from the engine and thus prevent the formation of ice.
Furthermore, thanks to the adoption of a new "fishtail" exhaust system, it was possible to obtain an additional 70 hp from the Merlin engine, which ensured an increase in the maximum speed to 579.36 km/h.

- To keep pace with technical advances and the capabilities required by operational needs, the Spitfire was produced in 46 versions, 33 land-based and 13 naval, seven of which were basic, with dozens of specific fittings.

Each version was identified by the designation Mk. (from the English Mark, model, type) followed by a Roman numeral up to version 20, and by Arabic numerals for subsequent versions, as the RAF changed its designation criteria in the post-war period.
In 1939 further improvements were added, bulletproof windshield, new and more powerful Merlin engine, self-sealing fuel tanks and, above all, new radio system with IFF (identification friend or foe) device.
The prototype K5054, was destroyed on landing on 4 September 1939 at Farnborough by Flight Lieutenant "Spinner" White, who died soon after.
The first production Spitfire, K9787, the first Mk.I differed somewhat from the prototype designed by Mitchell, who had in the meantime died of cancer - aged 42 - on 11 June 1937.
His successor, the expert engineer Joseph Smith, together with his team of over one hundred people, including engineers and designers, continued to work on its development until 1947, making several modifications.

- Most important was the new, stronger wing structure which now allowed the Spitfire to dive at speeds of up to 756 km/h.

The flaps had increased capacity, and the fuel tank capacity had increased by 12%, from 284 to 318 litres.
A new "teardrop" canopy gave the driver more room.
Later, the two-bladed wooden propeller, fitted to the first 75 aircraft produced, would be replaced by a three-bladed De Havilland two-pitch propeller.
Such a propeller would have increased the Spitfire's speed only marginally, but would have raised its maximum ceiling by 3,000 feet (914 meters), albeit at a slight reduction in its rate of climb of 14%, from 2,500 feet (771 meters) to 2,200 feet (663 meters) per minute.
The landing gear was high off the ground and had a very narrow track, with pivot points located under the fuselage.

- The mechanics of the trolley were also rudimentary, with a hand pump requiring 48 turns to ensure retraction.

The cockpit featured a Bakelite seat, transparent Perspex parts and fairly conventional controls, mainly a centrally located 'spade'-gripped control bar linked to steel cable-operated controls.
The ailerons were of the Frise type, without trim, but the trailing edge could be adjusted only once on the ground.
The rudder and elevator were moved by chains closed by steel cables, duplicated for safety, and crossed to obtain the correct movement of the elevator.
On the tail controls the pilot could also act with the trims to adjust the flight settings, while it is interesting to note that the tail controls were metal, but both the rudder and the elevators were covered in fabric.

- The Mk.I had a simple two-bladed wooden, fixed-pitch propeller.

It was cheap and weighed just 37 kg, but it was certainly not ideal for such a high-performance aircraft; in fact, variable-pitch propellers have a better performance because they adapt the incidence of the blade to the various flight conditions: high pitch value for take-off and climb and low for cruising, with just an aerodynamic nose cone covering the propeller hub.

Armor was absent for both the driver and the tanks, a solution adopted in order to have a lightweight structure that would not compromise performance.
Equipped with two flaps (trailing edge flaps) per wing, all-metal with two positions: open/closed.
They could not be used for take-off phases, but this was made possible only with the navalized version: the Seafire, thanks to the installation at an intermediate position of 18°.
The hydraulic system consisted of an engine-driven pump at 1,800 psi pressure and was used for the undercarriage only from the Mk.II onwards.

- The pneumatic system had two cylinders and operated brakes, flaps, weapons and other devices.

There were two fuel tanks: 218 and 168 litres, for a total of 386 litres, placed one above the other in the middle of the fuselage, just in front of the cockpit.
They were originally unprotected, but were later both protected and supplemented by additional external units, up to a maximum of 773 litres, with the possibility of further increasing the provision thanks to an internal tank, located in the long rear fuselage element, with another 132 litres.
The engine was a Merlin V12, originally running on 87 octane fuel and later, experimenting with higher compression ratios, on 130-150 octane fuel.

- The radiator was located under the starboard wing and used a mixture of 70% water and 30% ethylene glycol, the tank of which was placed behind the propeller, while the lubricating oil was stored in a tank located under the engine, where the carburetor air intake was also located.

Also standard was the provision of instruments such as a radio transceiver and at least two oxygen tanks for high-altitude flight.
At the time (mid 1930s) neither system was common on fighters.
The performance of the Mk.I was high to the point of achieving around 590 km/h speed at medium altitude, which was coupled with excellent handling and heavy armament.

The Spitfire was a revolutionary aircraft for 1936 and the scope for development would, sooner or later, overcome almost all of its youthful limitations and defects.
The first deliveries began in May 1938.
The first unit to be equipped with the new fighter was No. 19 Group based at Duxford, which received its first Spitfire (K9789) on 4 August 1938, replacing its Gauntlet biplanes.
The first RAF pilot to fly it was Squadron Leader Henry Cozens, who started out flying a Sopwith Camel and ended up flying the Vampire jet.

- But the Spitfire, Cozens claimed, was by far the best aircraft he had flown in the war.

By mid-September 1938, only five more aircraft had joined the first.
By early 1939, however, delivery times were increasing rapidly and by 3 September 1939, the day the UK entered the war with Germany, nine RAF and Auxiliary Air Force units, namely Nos. 19, 41, 54, 65, 66, 72, 74, 602 and 611 Groups (based at Duxford, Hornchurch, Church Fenton, Catterick and Abbotschurch), were fully equipped with Spitfires.

- Up to that point, 306 Mk.Is had been delivered.

Of these, however, 36 had been lost in training accidents.
Inevitably, RAF pilots coming to the Spitfire after training on biplanes such as the Tiger Moth or trainers such as the Miles Magister and Master, were involved in many accidents.
On take-off, visibility was hampered by the long nose and to move on the ground the pilots had to proceed in a zigzag pattern.
On landing, too many forgot to lower the landing gear, others failed to control the Spitfire's tendency to "float" on the runway.

- During violent maneuvers, above 4-5 G, the pilots' vision began to blur and the Supermarine fighter could reach 10 G.

Accustomed to Hawker Furys, they felt claustrophobic inside the Spitfire's closed cockpit, fearing that scratches, condensation

and oil drips from the Merlin engines on the Perspex panels might hinder visibility in combat.
Furthermore, the narrow undercarriage made night flying difficult and the Spitfire was used intermittently in this role, so much so that, as in the case of carrier-based employment, it never had full success, unlike the slower and more robust Hurricane.
The first aircraft to be decommissioned was one from XIX Squadron, lost on 16 August 1938 during a landing when an undercarriage failure caused it to roll over.
The pilot, Gordon Sinclair of IX Squadron, escaped unharmed and despite the unenviable distinction of having destroyed the first Spitfire, he would go on to become an ace with 10 confirmed aerial victories during 1940 both over Dunkirk and in the defence of England.
On 6 September 1939, Spitfires piloted by Paddy Byrne and John Freeborn of 74 Squadron, led by future ace Adolph Gysbert Malan, shot down the first aircraft over the River Medway in Kent.

- In a case of "friendly fire", known to history as the "Battle of Barking Creek", the two fighters shot down were Hurricanes from 56 Squadron.

Officer Montague Hulton-Harrop was killed.
An inquiry blamed the incident on a defect in the RAF's "radar control" system and the Spitfire pilots were cleared of any responsibility.
The accident, however, led to the installation of the IFF (Identification Friend or Foe) identification device, the forerunner of today's transponder.
The first enemy aircraft were shot down seven weeks later, on 16 October, when Spitfires of 603 Squadron shot down two Junkers Ju 88 bombers of 1/KG 30, led by Hauptmann Helmuth Pohle, over Rosyth, near the Firth of Forth, where German bombers had attacked HMS Southampton and HMS Edinburgh.
The first aerial victory by Spitfires based in England took place when 41 Squadron, taking off from Catterick, shot down a Heinkel He 111 near Whitby.

The RAF refused to send Spitfires to France during the crisis of early 1940.
They were still few in number, logistics were insufficient and the front was moving so quickly that they could have been caught by Blitzkrieg forces.
Only when the British Expeditionary Force was about to be trapped around Dunkirk did Fighter Command send its new fighters across the Channel, where they clashed with the Bf 109s.

- The first RAF pilot believed to have shot down a single-engined Messerschmitt was New Zealander Alan Christopher Deere of 54 Squadron on 23 May 1940, over Calais Marck airfield, followed soon after by his wingman Johnny Allen.

But in the fighting over Dunkirk, the RAF, trying to prevent the Luftwaffe from bombing the beaches while the troops embarked, lost 67 valuable Spitfires.
Pilots who had fought over France and survived had, however, learned a few useful "tricks" about how to deal with Messerschmitts.
One was to adjust the ground machine guns to focus their fire on a point 250 yards ahead of the wings, instead of the official 400.
During the months of the phoney war (a strange war is the definition of a historical period, during the Second World War, which goes from the end of the Polish campaign to the start of operations in France, and which marked a substantial standstill in the military operations of the conflict) there were desperate attempts to make the Spitfire fully operational, which began the war with limitations in terms of efficiency and operability, with a production level that was still insufficient.
The modifications devised were many and of considerable value.

- The climb to 6,100 meters originally took about 9.5 minutes, at maximum operating weight, and the practical ceiling was about 9,700 meters.

Although the Spitfire's cockpit was cramped, the availability of a lowering hatch on the port side made entry easy, without the need for the complicated manoeuvre of climbing over the side, especially with the flight gear which at the time included a parachute at buttock height.
Getting into the Spitfire certainly felt a sense of constraint for the average pilot, especially in the early model with its straight canopy, which also obstructed rearward visibility and could neither be opened in flight at speeds above 170 mph nor released in an emergency.
It came as no surprise to anyone, therefore, that within a few months it was replaced by a new, more comfortable, rounded model, and then integrated with a rear-view mirror installed above the windshield.
The reduction of a few km/h in speed in exchange for such improvements was deemed irrelevant.

- The flight controls were simple and in the centre of the cockpit there was the classic 'shovel' joystick with a sort of circle at the end, and a few buttons including the fire button.

The control panel had a dozen clock instruments for the analog presentation of the main flight data.
The throttle was on the left.
The sight was originally a simple reticle placed in front of the windshield.
The seat was a simple object made of Bakelite, with padding for the pilot's head. Initially it was not armored, nor was the windshield.
By operating the externally powered electric starter (replaced, from the Mk.II model onwards, by an explosive cartridge system) the machine was ready and the propeller was rapidly brought up to maximum revs.
Taxiing was quite easy, as the nose was relatively short compared to other machines and although it was still necessary to zig-zag, visibility was not excessively compromised, although the Hurricane was noticeably better thanks to the more elevated position of the pilot.

As mentioned, the initial propeller, a two-bladed wooden propeller with fixed pitch, was too limited to exploit the power, even though it was light (37 kg) and economical.

- The take-off run, almost 400 metres, was very high for a fighter, while the narrow landing gear track could lead to serious errors during taxiing and take-off.

The adoption of a three-bladed two-pitch metal propeller was an improvement and reduced the take-off run by about 100 meters, but the transition between speed performance and climb/close combat was not optimal, the engine being limited to a system with only two "gears".
Only the adoption of a constant-speed propeller finally made the machine suitable for all uses, even at the cost of a weight of 227 kg.
The manual oil pump in the early models caused problems in operation because the pilot was already busy holding the plane for take-off, and there was little room to move his hands, so much so that they tended to get sore when operating the pump 48 times and retracting the landing gear.
This problem was also later solved with a hydraulic system driven by the engine.

- To achieve improvements, the new 1,030 hp Merlin III engine was installed in place of the Merlin II at 4,353 meters.

This powerplant had a shaft suitable for three-bladed propellers such as the Rotol or the de Havilland two-position which increased speed by 5 mph.
For this reason the Rotol three-bladed constant speed propeller was soon adopted.
It weighed a whopping 228 kg, but adjusted the angle of incidence of the propeller blades optimally for each speed.
The takeoff run was further reduced to about 200 meters, and the climb to 6,100 meters was reduced to about 7 minutes and 42 seconds with a weight of 2,138-2,750 kg.
Maximum speed was reduced to 565 km/h, but the new aircraft became superior in everything else: agility, ceiling and climb.

Soon an IFF (Identification Friend or Foe) system was also adopted, weighing about 18 kg, which was absolutely essential if one wanted to conduct an air battle controlled by radar and radio links.

- More weight was added with armor.

First a 38mm armored glass windshield was installed, because, as Air Marshal Dowding said, if Chicago gangsters have armored windshields, my pilots must have them, too.
Then more armor plates were installed.
Initially, the only protection in this regard was the driver's armoured seat, which could protect him only from the critical rear attack sector.
The weight of the seat was 33 kg.
Rear view mirrors also appeared during 1940.

- 100-octane fuel, imported from the United States, replaced the 87-octane fuel, allowing for an increase in compression ratio and, therefore, power.

With a small modification to the engine and the new fuel it was possible to deliver up to 1,300 hp, for 5 minutes at most.
The maximum boost pressure increased from 2.7 to 5.5 kg and this allowed to improve the speed below the maximum normal value altitude (5,030 meters), 40 km/h more at sea level and 55 km/h at 3,050 metres.

- The tanks were covered with a layer of protective material.

These were just in front of the cockpit, and if they were hit by bullets during a fight they tended to catch fire, destroying the plane and endangering the pilot's life; it could happen, in fact, that the burning petrol reached the cockpit even without the tanks exploding.
It was a thin 3mm layer of light aluminum alloy, much smaller than you might expect, but weight limits did not allow for more.
The Hispano Suiza guns weighed less than the Browning machine gun group, but due to the friction caused by the muzzles, which protruded from the leading edge of the wing, they reduced the maximum speed by 5 km/h.

- The rudder pedal was also structured with two positions.

The normal one and the combat one, which was 15 cm higher and allowed the pilot to better resist violent maneuvers, which were capable of causing temporary loss of sight with this fighter.
The accelerations that the pilot could tolerate had increased by at least 1 G without loss of efficiency.

The Tangent Quota

The ceiling is that altitude, referred to the standard atmosphere model, beyond which an aircraft no longer has propulsive equilibrium, that is, the available power is less than the necessary power in the case of propellers, and the available traction is less than the necessary traction in the case of turbojets.
This does not mean that the aircraft cannot reach altitudes above the ceiling, but that it cannot do so in straight, horizontal flight conditions.

Theoretical tangency

The power delivered by an aircraft engine, due to the progressive rarefaction of the air, tends to decrease as the altitude increases, while the power required to maintain an aircraft in level flight increases.
There is an altitude at which the maximum power available from the engine is equal to the minimum power required for the aircraft to maintain level flight.
This altitude is called the theoretical tangency altitude because the curves of the power delivered and the power required as a function of the flight speed, plotted for this specific altitude, are tangent.
This point represents the only possible speed value for flight at tangent altitude.

Practical tangency

In case of climbing flight, with the decrease of the excess power, that is of the difference between the power delivered by the engine and the power required to maintain the aircraft in level flight conditions, a decrease in the rate of climb is observed since, approaching the theoretical tangency altitude, this rate tends to zero and, consequently, the time taken by the aircraft to reach this condition is theoretically infinite.

- The concept of practical ceiling is therefore introduced as the ceiling at which the aircraft still has sufficient excess power to climb at a speed of 100 ft/min (0.508 m/s).

The ceiling of an airplane depends on its characteristics.
For example, the Concorde had a high ceiling, higher than that of normal civil aircraft, because it was specifically designed to exploit the rarefaction of the air at high altitudes to reach supersonic speeds.
High ceilings could also be achieved thanks to the pressurization of aircraft cabins: for example, the World War II B-29 Superfortress bomber was the first pressurized aircraft in history and could easily escape enemy attacks by reaching an altitude that neither anti-aircraft guns nor Japanese fighters were able to reach.
In Europe, however, the Germans had aircraft, such as the Me-262 or the Komet, which could easily outrun enemy formations in altitude.

Technique

In 1934, Mitchell and the design staff decided to use a semi-elliptical wing shape to solve two conflicting requirements; the wing had to be thin to avoid creating too much drag, but it had to be thick enough to accommodate the retractable landing gear, armament, and ammunition.

- An elliptical planform is the most efficient aerodynamic shape for an untwisted wing, leading to the least amount of induced drag.
- The ellipse was tilted so that the center of pressure, which occurs at the quarter-chord position, aligned with the main spar, preventing the wings from twisting.

The elliptical wing was a direct result of Mitchell's request for a wing thin, but thick enough, and structurally strong enough, where it met the fuselage to accommodate weapons and retracted landing gear.
The number of 303 Brownings had, in fact, risen to eight, following the recommendations of Squadron Leader Ralph Sorely of the Air Ministry's Operational Requirements, so the wing had to be long enough to accommodate them.

- The ellipse was simply the shape that allowed for the thinnest possible wing, with room inside to carry the necessary structure. And it looked good.

The wing section used was of the NACA 2200 series, which had been adapted to create a thickness-to-chord ratio of 13% at the root, reduced to 9.4% at the tip.

- A 6° dihedral was adopted to give greater lateral stability.

A feature of the wing that contributed greatly to its success was an innovative spar arm design, consisting of five square tubes that fit into each other.
As the wing tapered across its span, tubes were progressively cut away in a leaf spring-like fashion: two of these arms were linked together by an alloy web, creating a light, very strong main spar.

The landing gear legs were attached to pivot points integral to the rear inner section of the main spar and retracted outward and slightly rearward into wells in the non-load-bearing wing structure.
The resulting narrow landing gear track was considered an acceptable compromise as it reduced bending loads on the main spar during landing.

- Forward of the spar, the wing's thick-skinned leading edge formed a strong, rigid D-shaped box, which supported most of the wing loads.

At the time the wing was designed, this D-shaped leading edge was intended to house vapor condensers for the evaporative cooling system intended for the PV-XII: however, ongoing problems with the evaporative system in the Goshawk led to the adoption of a cooling system using 100% glycol.
The radiators were housed in a new radiator duct designed by Fredrick Meredith of the Royal Aircraft Establishment (RAE) at Farnborough, Hampshire.
This used cooling air to generate thrust, greatly reducing the net drag produced by the radiators: in turn, the leading edge structure lost its condenser function, but was later adapted to accommodate integral fuel tanks of various sizes.
Airflow through the main radiator was controlled by pneumatic outlet flaps.
On early models of the Spitfire (Mk I to Mk VI), the single flap was operated manually using a lever to the left of the pilot's seat.
When the two-stage Merlin was introduced in the Spitfire Mk IX, the radiators were split to make room for an intercooler radiator; the radiator under the starboard wing was halved in size and the intercooler radiator was housed alongside it.

- Under the port wing, a new radiator fairing housed a square oil cooler alongside the other half-radiator unit: the two radiator flaps were now operated automatically by a thermostat.

In later years, Shenstone was always keen to repeat that the Spitfire's famous wing was not copied from that of the elegant

Heinkel He 70, a small mail plane and potential dive bomber for the Luftwaffe, which first flew in 1932.
In fact, Rolls-Royce was so enthusiastic about the He 70's potential as a flying platform for experimental engines that it sent a team to Germany to purchase one.
And the German government approved the deal, but only in exchange for a number of Rolls-Royce Kestrel engines.

- The elliptical shape reduced the curvature of the wings to the tip, causing airflow to be uniform along the entire length and near-zero thrust at the tip, all of which improved aerodynamic efficiency.

Another feature of the wing was its "washout".
The trailing edge of the wing twisted slightly upwards along its span, the angle of incidence decreased from +2° at the root to -1/2° at the tip.
This caused the wing roots to stall before the tips, reducing tip stall that could otherwise cause the wing to flop, often leading to a spin.
As the wing roots began to stall, the separating airflow would begin to buffet (vibrate) the aircraft, warning the pilot, allowing even relatively inexperienced pilots to fly the aircraft at the limits of its performance.

- This washout was first seen on the wing of the Type 224 and became a consistent feature in subsequent designs leading to the Spitfire.

The complex design of the wing, particularly the precision required to manufacture the vital spar and leading edge structures, caused some major delays in Spitfire production early on.
Problems increased when the work was handed over to subcontractors, most of whom had never dealt with metal-framed high-speed aircraft: however, by June 1939, most of these problems had been resolved and production was no longer hampered by the lack of wings.
Its use, however, has remained limited for several reasons:

- The manufacture of elliptical components is difficult and expensive.

- The pure elliptical shape is a myth. A truncated ellipse can be just as effective, while a trapezoidal wing, which is easier to produce, is very close in effectiveness.
- The uniform thrust across the entire wing increased the risk of stalling at low speed.

The armament nomenclature in the Spitfire has a certain rationality and ease of reading.
In fact, there are 4 different types of wing (intended as wing armament): type A, B, C, E.
The D was unarmed and contained fuel.
The standard armament fitted to the so-called "A Wing" was eight 7.7 mm Browning machine guns, each carrying 300 rounds, positioned to fire outside the propeller disc, in a wing battery collimated to focus the burst some distance from the nose, for a total of nearly 17 seconds of fire.
The first Spitfires were delivered, however, with only four machine guns, because there was a shortage of Brownings.
The other four were installed later.
Pilots, from the very first clashes in the Battle of Britain, complained about this armament which was decidedly ineffective against the bombers, which were able to return to base despite having been riddled with bullets, evidently too light.
As for dogfights against Bf 109s, however, it was quite good, thanks above all to its high rate of fire.

- Firing tests showed that the Brownings worked perfectly both on the ground and at low altitude, but that the extreme cold at high altitude tended to freeze the guns, especially the outer ones.

Since the machine guns fired from an open hatch, cold air flowed into the barrel unimpeded : a heating system had to be devised, with ducts channelling air from the engine radiator to the guns, and compartments to trap the hot air in the wing.
Red cloth patches were used to protect the weapons from cold, moisture and dirt until they were fired, which, moreover, allowed a few kilometres to be gained in top speed by reducing aerodynamic drag.

In the spring of 1940, the "De Wilde" incendiary rounds were introduced, which approximately doubled the effectiveness of the .303 Browning rounds. They were much appreciated by pilots because their bright flash on impact gave clear confirmation that they were hitting the target.
In June 1939, a 20 mm Hispano cannon, with a 60-round drum magazine, was fitted to each wing, replacing two of the four Browning machine guns.

- Known as the 'B' wing, this wing was tested on an early production Spitfire Mk.I in February 1939 and consisted of 2 x 20 mm Hispano cannon (with 60 rounds each) and 4 x 7.7 mm Brownings (with 350 rounds each).

This aircraft became the prototype of the Spitfire IB of which 30 were delivered by August 1940 for experimental trials.
However, in service they were not fully appreciated and were withdrawn as the drum magazine, after a few shots, caused the gun to jam, in addition to having few rounds, sufficient for only 5 seconds of fire.
The frequent jams were due mainly to the fact that the wing was not rigid enough for the Hispano, but also to the mounting of the cannons on one side, in order to contain the magazine with the rounds as much as possible in the wing.
In January 1940, Pilot Officer George Proudman used the prototype with cannons in combat, but had to report that the starboard gun had jammed after firing a single shot, while the port gun had fired 30 rounds before jamming.
Coincidentally a Dornier Do 17 was shot down by a cannon-armed Spitfire in early March 1940.

- In June 1940 the first cannon-armed Spitfires were supplied to 19 Squadron, but the Hispanos proved highly unreliable and if one jammed, the recoil of the other would knock the aircraft sideways, adversely affecting aim.

In combat the gun proved so unreliable that the 19th requested an exchange of its aircraft for the more worn, but machine-gun-armed, ones from an operational training unit.

The swap was made in September, but in the previous month Supermarine had perfected a more effective gun installation with an improved feed mechanism.
The drum loading system was replaced by a belt loading system, based on the design of the Frenchman Chatellerault, in order to increase the quantity of ammunition available.
From October onwards, the British company delivered the new aircraft (also equipped with four wing-mounted machine guns) to the 19th, which used them in combat.

- The belt mechanism, however, which used a spring kept loaded by recoil, added an additional 8 kg to the weight of the weapon which normally weighed 50 kg.

But the reliability of the Hispano was never high.
Normally they jammed every 1,500 shots, but on makeshift, dusty airfields, such as those on the beaches of Normandy and the desert, the average was halved.
Furthermore, at the ever-increasing altitudes reached by the Spitfires, they were more prone to icing-on-the-floor malfunctions than the Brownings.

- The "C" type wing was also called "universal", as it gave the flexibility to mount two different armament options: 2 guns plus 4 machine guns or 4 guns.

Armament could be changed directly on the airfield and in a relatively short time.
The new Hispano Mk IIs were adopted which gave the possibility of doubling the number of rounds (now 120 per gun).
The combination of 2 cannons and 4 machine guns was used most, which gave at the same time a high rate of fire and excellent fire potential.

- The "D" wing was used on the Spitfire to increase its range, as it mounted a 66 gallon (300 liters) fuel tank forward of the wing. To prevent the fuel from expanding under heat and damaging the wing, safety valves, with small external vent pipes, were fitted near the wing tips.
- The "E" type wing was derived from the C type wing, of which it retained the main structure.

The machine gun slots were closed, the 20 mm gun was moved further back, so it appeared more streamlined, and the other gun slot was occupied by a 0.50 (12.7 mm) heavy machine gun.

- This resulted in a total armament of 2 Hispanos with 120 rounds each, sufficient for 11 seconds of fire, and 2 12.7 mm (0.50 in) Brownings with 250 rounds each, sufficient for 18 seconds of fire.

The later versions of the Spitfire (starting with the Mk.21) had a completely redesigned wing.
The wing structure was revised, larger ailerons to increase roll, slightly different wingtips which slightly modified the typical ellipticity of the wing.
In addition, a new, taller landing gear was designed to allow the use of large counter-rotating propellers: it was completely faired when closed in flight.

- The armament consisted of 4 Hispano guns (Mk II or Mk V): it was never designated with a letter, it was called "new wing".

The most cost-effective solution was to have two 20 mm cannons in the innermost positions and four 7.7 mm machine guns in the outermost ones, with about 300 rounds each.
This gave different results depending on the firing range: for the first 6 seconds the Spitfire could massacre anything in its sights, given the power of the Hispano: then, however, it was left with only four 7.7 mm, which were scarcely effective.
The Macchi 202, for example, was equipped with 2 12.7 mm guns, but with a high fire autonomy (theoretically up to 400 rounds each, in practice 350-370), so that it had the possibility of delivering continuous fire for about 40 seconds, and what's more from the most suitable position, that of the guns in the nose, with a natural and instinctive aim, even without using the S. Giorgio reflex system.
The Spitfire had all its weapons in the wings, which placed them outside the propeller disc, a significant gamble as it meant installing them all a considerable distance from the fuselage.

- Stability and concentration of shooting had to be taken care of as best as possible.

On the other hand, there was no limitation to their rate of fire and the large number of guns on board was sufficient for effective shooting and to hit any target with a large number of shots; but without the 20 mm it was not superior to the firepower of the Macchi, and was even at a disadvantage if the latter had the two additional 7.7 mm, rarely carried since they increased the weight by about 100 kg.
The Macchi was lightly armed and at the same time heavy, so it is not surprising that it was also a stable firing platform, thanks also to the concentration of weapons in the nose or at most, in the inner part of the wings (moreover they were 7.7 mm weapons).

- For a greater margin of superiority the Spitfire had to wait, further weighing down, the belt guns, with 120 rounds and, therefore, 12 seconds of fire, a much more comfortable margin (6 bursts of 2 seconds, for example).

Against the Bf-109 too, the verdict was far from unanimous.
The Bf-109F was the equivalent of the Spitfire and had 150 15 or 20 mm rounds, plus two 7.92 mm guns.
The firepower of the heavy machine guns was about 12 seconds, so even here, against the Spitfire , the disadvantage was less than it might seem: there was only one gun, but with double the firepower, until the arrival of the Spitfire Mk.VC.

- When the 20 mm ammunition ran out, both fighters could have small arms at their disposal, but the Bf-109 had only two to the Spitfire's four.

In fact, as armament, the Spitfire had the same armament in each wing that the Bf-109F had in total.
As can be seen, the number and caliber of firearms was paid for by a reduced firepower, which made it necessary to place the on-board bursts with great precision.
The 12.7 mm was, however, a tricky customer because it was powerful enough to penetrate robust structures such as the longerons and the armor plating protecting the pilot of many aircraft.

The British should have known this, as American aircraft, given their faith in the M2, a powerful but rather heavy weapon, were all armed with these machine guns.

- The P-40s were rather clumsy, but with 4 or 6 M2s and a good supply of rounds, about 300 per gun, they were capable of causing enormous damage to anything in the air that they could aim at.

The Soviets interpreted the matter in their own way, replacing the Hurricane's machine guns (many were given as a backup) with six 12.7 mm guns, sometimes with a seventh turned backwards for self-defense. In contrast, the P-40s, which remained used primarily as fighters, were lightened, often limited to just two M2s.

- In terms of firepower, the Spitfire Mk.V had a six-second burst for the 20 mm and about 35 seconds for the 7.7 mm: a two-second burst equals 40 20 mm and 133 7.7 mm rounds, equal to 11.3 kg of which an appreciable portion was explosive.
- The Bf-109F-2 could fire 25 15 mm and 67 7.92 mm rounds, equal to 5.2 kg.
- The Macchi MC202 approximately 36 12.7 mm or 1,300 grams, approximately, of which a maximum of about 30 of HE (pentrite), or as much as 3 or 4 20 mm shots could fire.

The destructive factor of these weapons has been calculated in various ways:

- Hurricane and Spitfire Mk.I of 160 (8 x 7.7 mm) with 1.7 kg of ammunition/s,
- The Bf-109E came in at 2.37 kg or a potential of 286.
- The Ki-61 with 20 mm guns reached 362.
- The P-40E at 360.
- The Macchi MC205 at 438.
- The P-47 at 480.
- The FW-190A-4 at 666.
- Up to 2,320 for the Me.262 (4 Mk 108).

The Spitfire Mk.VC with four 20 mm guns could fire 10 kg/s bursts for twelve seconds.
There was also a progressive increase in armour, which on the Mk.VC model became 87.6 kg total, including for the magazines for the 20 mm guns and for the coolant in the tank behind the propeller.
Soon engines such as the low-altitude Merlin 50 and 55 appeared, producing up to 1,585 hp, and mounts for two 113 kg or one 227 kg bombs.
Among the innovations that the Spitfire introduced in its early forms was the adoption of entirely metal ailerons, instead of the fabric-covered ones: the latter were easier to build and lighter, but they were also, paradoxically, "heavy" when it came to flying at high speed, because they tended to swell and block the controls, especially above 600 km/h.

- This did not stop the Spitfires from launching into fearsome dives, with speeds of up to 960 km/h (600 mph) being recorded as early as 1940.

If this measurement had been accurate, which was not necessarily the case, the instruments of the time were not exactly precision, it was an exceptional value, still sufficient to catch the Bf-109s after a chase started from high altitude.
The Spitfire managed to prove itself aerodynamically superior to its rival, exceeding it in peak speed and recovering the initial disadvantage. But the controls were not tested for these experiments: the ailerons were one of them.
It is not clear how many degrees per second of roll rate they allowed, and how much lightness compared to normal controls, but it is known what effect they had.
Douglas Bader launched an attack on a formation of Bf-109s, only to be called off by his comrades who radioed: *"We can't follow you, we don't have those damned metal ailerons yet."*
So, Bader managed, in those fast maneuvers, to distance his formation not homogeneously equipped. Who knows if later, his downing was not also determined by this.
One problem with the effectiveness of the ailerons, however, was that the Spitfire's single-spar wing was not strong enough to withstand the action of these systems and the control reversal

speed, originally intended to be around 930 km/h, was quickly reached.
Only the F Mk 21 would be able to take it to over 1,100 km/h.

- The ailerons were of the Frise type, they were not equipped with trim, but the trailing edge could be adjusted on the ground only once.

The rudder and elevator were moved by closed chains of steel cables, duplicated for safety, and crossed to obtain the correct movement of the elevator: on the tail controls the pilot could also act with the trims to adjust the flight attitude.
The flaps (trailing edge flaps), entirely metal, were two per wing, and had only two positions, open or completely closed: they could not be used for take-off, while this was made possible with the navalized version, the Seafire, thanks to the installation of an intermediate position of 18°.
The hydraulic system featured an engine-driven pump with 1,800 psi of pressure, and was used for the bogie only from the MkII onwards.
There were two fuel tanks: 218 and 168 litres, placed one above the other in the middle of the fuselage, just in front of the cockpit.
Originally they were unprotected, but were later both protected and supplemented by additional external units, up to a maximum of 773 litres, with the possibility of further increasing the provision thanks to an internal tank, located in the long rear fuselage element, with another 132 litres.

Technical Features

Dimensions and weights

- Length: 9.12 meters
- Wingspan: 11.23 meters
- Height: 3.86 meters
- Wing area: 22.48 m^2
- Empty weight: 2,309 kg
- Load weight: 3,004 kg
- Maximum take-off weight: 3,071 kg

Propulsion

- Engine: One Rolls-Royce Merlin Mk.45
- Power: 1,470 hp (1,096 kW)

Performance

- Maximum speed: 594 km/h
- Climb speed: 19.7 m/sec
- Autonomy: 1,827 km
- Tangency: 11,300 meters

Armament

- Machine guns: 4 Browning 7.7 mm caliber
- Guns: 2 Hispano 20 mm caliber
- Bombs: 2 x 113 kg

The Battle of Britain

When the Battle of Britain began on 12 August 1940, there were around 250 Spitfires in service on the front line, against 350 Hurricanes, there were also Defiants, Blenheims and a few Gladiators.

On the other side 2,500 German aircraft, of which at least a thousand Bf-109s.

The figures, however, only refer to front-line units, and not to reserve aircraft: the Spitfire Mk.I alone produced 1,500 aircraft, the Hurricane Mk.I 2,300.

- Thus, there was no shortage of reserve aircraft: the RAF's order of battle featured 19 Squadron of Spitfire Is.

The Spitfire became the iconic fighter of the Battle of Britain, but the Germans did not actually owe most of their losses to them: strangely enough, the Hurricanes alone shot down more aircraft than all other defensive systems put together by the British.

It was obviously also more widespread than the Spitfire, and also suffered greater losses.

Perhaps its good fortune was that it was often tasked with engaging enemy bombers while the Spitfires took care of the fighters, but in practice this often did not work out that way.

The Hurricane was used wherever it could be sent, and its stability of fire, apparently greater than that of the Spitfire, as well as its robustness, helped it greatly in destroying bombers with prolonged and effective bursts.

But it wasn't easy: often enemy bombers returned to base with more than 200 bullet holes, so the problem wasn't so much this, nor the poor aim of the British fighters.

In any case, it was difficult to expect more than 5-10% of the bullets to hit the target.

- The problem of the Battle of Britain, however, was not so much technical as tactical.

It was thought that the bombers that would move towards the national territory would be without escort, when the war broke out in a future that sooner or later would come, given the rearmament programs, which had become desperately inexorable after 1938 (when the world finally began to understand the 'tractability' of Nazi-fascism).
The sudden collapse of France was not expected.
But it happened.
Besides, the Germans did not even plan to attack Great Britain so massively.
The Bf-110 was their main asset, but it proved to be unmanageable against RAF fighters, as it had in France: so the success it had in Poland as the main LW fighter was not to be repeated.
The Bf-109s were needed, but they did not have enough range: unfortunately for the Germans, the version that would have been needed, the E-7, arrived only in September, too late.
With 400 litres internally but also 300 in an external tank, it would have been the fighter that was needed for air combat, increasing the reduced range of 250 km, 660 km of autonomy at typical cruising speed.
The RAF fighters did not have good tactics: they still flew in three-man formation, with the two wingmen covering the leader's back, but in doing so they were too focused on their task and too vulnerable to attacks from behind.
The Germans had the basic formations of two (pair) and four aircraft (section), which were much more operationally flexible.

- The Germans already had their plans: the attacker always has an initial advantage over the defender, and so it was possible for them to organize, without the defenders' knowledge, large-scale raids: without radar, they would have been deadly and unstoppable.

But strangely, despite an initial attack with BF-110s, the Germans gave up on destroying the British radar sites. Yet it would not have been difficult: antennas over 100 meters high could not be hidden.
The initial action hit 5 stations and destroyed one, but ended there also due to the losses suffered.

The Germans had air defense radar, but, as difficult as it may seem to understand, they did not carry out this type of attack: rather , in July they lost dozens of aircraft attacking coastal traffic.
The Battle officially began around mid-August 1940, but it is an indicative date, because fighting had been going on since before. Only that at a certain point, having lost all hope of making Great Britain surrender or come to terms, Hitler wanted to use a heavy hand: after all, it was the English who had hit Berlin since May.
In the period between 10 July and 31 October 1940, also due to the RAF's overly rigid tactics compared to the extremely flexible German schemes, 352 Spitfires were lost, with a victory/loss ratio slightly negative compared to the Bf 109 (1.4:1):

- 242 Spitfires shot down by Bf 109s versus 168 Bf 109s shot down by Spitfires.

Thus, in this frantic battle, which should have confirmed Douhetti's theories of air warfare as a decisive weapon, thousands of young men died chasing each other with their planes armed with machine gun batteries. The myth was born, that of "never so many owed so much to so few", but at what a price. Even on the ground the English suffered losses and damages not indifferent, but they were not defeated.
It was not just the few pilots who determined this: the control rooms, the airmen, the workers and the technicians who churned out huge quantities of aircraft and equipment were the submerged part of the iceberg: the British population, feeling anything but helpless thanks to their airmen, managed to accept with spirit the worst bombing campaign ever carried out in Europe, and, in terms of material intensity, in the world.

- In the end, everything was decided by industrial capacity: so many Spitfires and Hurricanes were built or repaired that British aviators never had a shortage of aircraft.

Rather, there was a shortage of pilots, between deaths and injuries: they could not be produced continuously.

But the Germans also lost airmen, and those who fell on missions were dead or taken prisoner, and therefore, lost. Not so for the British.

- The German “Rotte”, or “loose” pair, consisted of only two aircraft, which were those of the leader of the pair and the wingman who acted as bodyguard.

It was much better, and even better was the Schwarme, two “Routes” that made a front of well-armed planes and that covered each other, with the ability to maneuver all to their best; instead, in the British three-man formation it was the formation leader who turned at will, while the wingmen were glued to his tail, and had to follow him, ending up not understanding well what was happening.

Aside from this, high-speed combat was not contemplated due to the excessive acceleration suffered by the body, so speed was seen mainly as a potential to approach and move away from the place of combat, rather than as a resource to be exploited.

It was tiring to fight like that, but the English pilots, especially because of the double pedals, showed that it could be done without too many problems. The Germans knew this without having to do any new experiments: they had already understood it fighting against the I-16s in Spain, where their Bf-109B and C were forced, willingly or not, not to get involved in close combat against the more agile and armed opponents, who were also only slightly inferior in speed.

The advantage of high altitude remained, and as Udet (ace of 1916) said, whoever has the most altitude wins, translated he has more energy stored away (altitude = potential energy) and can use it for dive attacks and then fast climbs to return to the "safe" altitude.

- The Spitfires and Hurricanes had greater agility and an armament more suited to attacking bombers, with a few guns of fairly high power, but a reduced rate of fire and range of fire.

The Bf-109Es, having exhausted the seven fateful seconds of fire allowed by the MG FFs, were left with only two MG 17s, too few to easily shoot down the targets, while the rate of fire

and speed of the bullets was not very suitable for combat against small and agile targets such as fighters.
The British aircraft's 8 Brownings were more effective against fighters, but ironically, their primary task was supposed to be to hit bombers.
All things considered, the Bf-109Es and Spitfires would have had to swap on-board weapons to really get things right.
The Bf-109s' armament would have been too small for the Spitfires, with their very capable wings; the Bf-109s' armament would have been too large, as they would have been unlikely to be able to accommodate as many weapons as the Spitfires.
The latter had their characteristic high nose, because the British engine had a conventional V-shaped cylinder, not an inverted one as in the case of the Bf-109s, which could thus afford two guns above the cowling.
Perhaps, counting also the third of the engine gun, it would have been possible to add two more per wing (instead of just one like the first BF-109s), given that they were capable of carrying two 20 mm MG FFs.
For the Spitfires it would have been child's play to accommodate two MG 17s and two MG FFs, while relying on just two guns was certainly not the best, especially considering the overall unreliability.
While the Hurricane was noticeably slower than other fighters, including the Bf-110, it was also more robust and capable of turning tighter, but with rather heavy controls and a rather slow climb, which remained around the levels of the early Spitfires, i.e. about 9 minutes to 6,100 meters.

- Compared to its main competitor, the Messerschmitt Bf 109, the Spitfire was faster and considerably more maneuverable, but the German fighter boasted more effective armament, could outperform its British opponent in climb rate and dive rate and could operate at higher altitudes.

The Spitfire Mk.I and the Messerschmitt Bf 109E nearly matched each other in speed below 6,000 meters.
The Supermarine fighter had a slight edge at lower altitudes but, above, the German fighter became progressively better.

At the outbreak of hostilities, the Bf. 109 was probably the best high-altitude fighter in the world:

- The Me 109's acceleration was better at all altitudes.
- Its "candle" climb and pull-up were better, though not by much.
- Its speed was 569.70 km/h (354 mph) at 3,750 meters, 12.87 km/h (8 mph) slower than the Spitfire.

But the Supermarine fighter's speed advantage could be deceptive.
At low altitudes the Me 109 was probably faster, and, in any case, the speed of each individual aircraft varied.
The German pilots, as Adolf Galland wrote in his " *The first and the last",* were convinced that the Bayerische Flugzeugwerke fighter was faster at most of the altitudes at which the clashes took place.
The Bf 109's ceiling was 11,430 meters, compared to 10,668 meters for the Spitfire, and its initial rate of climb was 945 meters per minute, compared to 750 meters per minute for the Spitfire.
The Spitfire's roll rate was better at low speeds, although this advantage diminished at speeds above 350 miles per hour (563.26 km/h).
Its turning ability was clearly better than that of the Messerschmitt, particularly at low altitude.
Maximum turn radius at 12,000 feet, at an air speed of 240 miles (386.24 km/h.) with both aircraft shaking at the stall threshold gave the following results:

- Turn radius: Spitfire 609 feet (185.62 meters), Me 109, 783 feet (238.65 meters).
- Rate of turn: Spitfire 33 degrees per second, Me 109, 26 degrees per second.

An important advantage enjoyed by the Bf 109 was the fact that its Daimler-Benz DB 601A engine was petrol-injected: this allowed the pilot to immediately launch his fighter into a dive, saving precious seconds.

- Conversely, the Spitfire's Merlin engine, being carburettor-equipped, could not be pushed into a dive directly from level flight, as the negative G thrust would have cut off the fuel flow, instantly stalling the engine.

At the beginning of the Battle of Britain the Germans captured four Spitfires.

"In Jever I was able to fly on one of them" , recalls Oberleutnant Hans Schmoller-Haldy, of Geschwader 54.
"My first impression was that it had a nice engine, the Bf 109's was very noisy. The Spitfire was also more maneuverable and easier to land. The Bf 109 did not forgive the slightest carelessness. I felt at ease with the Spitfire straight away, but my impression was that the 109 was faster, especially in a dive. And the visibility was better: in the Spitfire you were very far back, just above the wings. Personally, I would never have exchanged my 109 for the English fighter."

In the Battle of Britain the Me 109 proved itself, shooting down more fighters than it lost.
This success was due in part to the adoption of better combat formations, the superior level of training of Luftwaffe pilots and the superior average quality of German fighters, the majority of those encountered by the British at the time being Hurricanes.
Luftwaffe fighter pilots flew in formations perfected in Spain and according to World War I principles, put into practice in the Spanish Civil War.

- The basic unit was the Rotte, consisting of two aircraft separated by about 200 yards.

In this way, each pilot could "cover the tail", that is, keep an eye on the other's "blind spots", although this remained the primary task of the wingman.
This basic unit could be easily enlarged by simply replicating it.
Two pairs made up a Schwarme and the four aircraft abreast were arranged just as the pilots of the great German ace Oswald Boelcke had done during the First World War, forming what was called the "four-fingered formation".

Several of these formations, echeloned, constituted a Staffel and flew in a wavering fashion back and forth for mutual protection. As for the Focke-Wulf, it was 25-30 miles per hour (40-48 km/h) faster than the Spitfire V at almost any altitude.
The arrival of this advanced BMW radial-engined fighter prompted Joseph Smith and his team at Supermarine to accelerate the development of the Spitfire to the maximum.
But for most of the year, and until the arrival of the Spitfire IX, the Fw dominated the skies.

"The Focke-Wulf 190 certainly shocked the British. This new fighter out-climbed and out-dived the Spitfire. Now, for the first time, the Germans were out-flying our pilots."

wrote Douglas Bader in his autobiography "Fight for the sky".

And they also surpassed them in armament.
Its roll rate, then, was incredibly fast, allowing it to change direction very quickly.

- An official RAF report from July 1942 revealed that when the FW was in a turn and was attacked by the Spitfire, the greater degree of bank allowed it to dart out into a turn in the opposite direction.

The Spitfire pilot had great difficulty following the manoeuvre, even when he was prepared to do so.
Only when turning did the Spitfire maintain the advantage, with its lighter wing loading.
But even this was not always guaranteed, because the FW 190 could turn very tightly using 10 degrees of flaps and using its blistering acceleration to compensate for the increased drag.
There are several accounts of FW 190s out-turning Spitfires, the best known of which is reported by ace Johnny Johnson in his book "Wing Leader", where he tells of a FW 190 giving him a very bad quarter of an hour over Dieppe.
When a Luftwaffe pilot landed his Fw 190A intact in South Wales in June 1942, comparative tests were carried out to devise the best methods of dealing with the new German fighter.

Spitfire pilots were advised to maintain a high cruising speed to reduce the chances of being intercepted.
As a method of evasion, the British pilot was advised to push the plane into a shallow dive, in case he saw the German plane in time.

- Had the pursuit continued, he would have been caught, but as about a mile was covered every ten seconds, such evasive action could be attempted with some hope of success.

The new fighter had a maximum speed of 656.61 km/h (408 mph).
It was well armed with two 7.92 mm machine guns firing through the propeller disc, two more at the wing roots, and a pair of 20 mm wing cannon.
With the Mk.IX, parity was achieved, with a speed of about 15 km/h lower at low altitude, but from 2,400 meters the Spitfire gradually gained the advantage, and the climb was even greater, especially above 6,700 meters.
This time the tangency was also about 2,000 meters higher.

Versions

Built in 20,351 examples and in approximately forty versions, the Supermarine Spitfire was the only aircraft to be produced throughout the entire duration of the Second World War.
The Spitfire was produced in dozens of versions and sub-versions, comprising thousands of aircraft belonging to at least three or four different generations.

- Slowly, almost every detail of the Spitfire was changed, strengthened or simply improved.

In effect, rather than a single type, it was a true family of aircraft, gradually adapted for every practical need, although the range was never sufficient for strategic offensive missions, for which, in any case, it had not been foreseen in the design phase.

Spitfire Mk.I

This was the first production version, entering service on 4 August 1938: the first Spitfire Mk.I flew on 14 May 1938 with 19 Squadron RAF at Duxford, subsequently assigned to nine operational squadrons by September 1939, and a further ten by mid-1940.

- 19 Squadron, one of the last surviving Battle of Britain squadrons, was disbanded on 24 November 2011, 96 years after it was first formed.

The disbandment event, held at RAF Valley, was led by General Kevin Marsh, the last commanding officer of 19 Squadron, and was attended by Chief of the Air Staff, Air Chief Marshal Sir Stephen Dalton, former Air Marshal Sir William Wratten and Lieutenant Ken Wilkinson who flew the Spitfire in the Battle of Britain with 19 Squadron.
Equipped with the Rolls-Royce Merlin II engine and eight 7.7 mm machine guns located in the wings, the Spitfire Mk.I were an operational aircraft, produced in 1,519 examples, which, during the tragic months of the Battle of Britain, were able to assert themselves despite the great mass of enemy aircraft.
The first 174 examples differed from the original prototype in some details: in fact, they were equipped with the 1,044 hp (768 kW) Merlin II engine, a two-bladed fixed-rate wooden propeller, no protective armour, maximum take-off weight of approximately 2,600 kg.

- On 87 octane fuel the Merlin II produced 1,030 hp (750 kW), but on 100 octane fuel it delivered 1,310 hp (977 kW) at 3,000 rpm at 9,000 ft (2,745 m).

This modification, costing £53 per aircraft, mainly concerned the compressor, which was now capable of giving a boost pressure of 0.84 kg/cm ^{2} rather than 0.44 kg/cm ^{2}.
The difference was colossal: the rate of ascent increased, and the climb became much more noticeable; furthermore, the

maximum speed increased by 40 km/h at sea level and by 55 km/h at 3,000 meters.

More importantly, the increased power compensated for the additional weight of the armor plates in front of and behind the pilot and the radio equipment installed on each aircraft.

Spitfire Mk.I

Main features of the Spitfire Mk.I were:

- Length 9.12 meters
- Wingspan 11.23 meters
- Height 3.74 meters
- Wing area 22.48 m^2
- Weight: 2,033 kg empty - 2,640 kg maximum take-off
- Maximum speed 582 km/h at 5,640 meters
- Climbed to 6,095 meters in 9'25"
- Tangency 9,724 meters
- Range 688 km at a cruising speed of 489 km/h.

The March 1940 Mk.I had the Merlin III engine rather than the II, the difference being that the power, 900 hp at take-off and 1,060 hp at altitude, was delivered at maximum level not at 5,200 meters, but at just 900 meters.

- Weight 2,138-2,745 kg

- Speed 568 km/h at 6,095 meters
- Climbed to 6,095 meters in 7.6 minutes
- Tangency 10,577 meters
- Dimensions identical to the previous model.

Also in 1940, 30 aircraft were designated Supermarine Spitfire Mk.IB, as they were equipped with two 20 mm Hispano cannon each (60-round drum magazine) in place of four of the machine guns, thus distinguishing themselves from the Supermarine Spitfire Mk.IA, which were equipped with the initial eight 7.7 mm machine guns.

From the 78th aircraft onwards, the two-bladed wooden fixed-pitch propeller was replaced by a de Havilland two-bladed two-pitch propeller (weighing 183 kg and with a diameter of 1.93 meters), allowing the aircraft to increase its maximum speed by 8 km/h, from 582 to 590 km/h, but at the cost of a decrease in the maximum climb rate, which went from 12.85 to 11.05 m/s.

Other substantial changes were the adoption of a curved cockpit canopy, which improved visibility for the pilot, the introduction of a glass shield placed in front of the windshield, armor plating behind the pilot, the adoption of self-sealing tanks (a fireproof coating called "Linatex", later replaced with a self-sealing rubber layer), and the replacement of the manual landing gear retraction system with a hydraulic device, as well as the tail wheel in place of the metal skid.

From the 175th example onwards another very important modification was introduced, consisting of the adoption of the Merlin III but capable of mounting a three-bladed constant-speed de Havilland propeller (weight 220 kg), which allowed for automatic adjustment of the pitch and consequently of the engine revolutions.

- This new propeller allowed a further general increase in performance, particularly in the field of climb rate (16.4 minutes to reach 900 meters, compared to 23.8 with the two-pitch propeller).

Also starting in September 1940, IFF (Identification Friend or Foe) equipment was fitted which weighed about 18 kg and could be identified by metal antennae fitted between the tailplane tips and the rear fuselage.

- Although the added weight and antennas reduced the top speed by about 3 km/h, it allowed the aircraft to be identified as a "friendly" on radar.

The lack of such equipment was a factor in the Battle of Barking Creek on 6 September 1939 when six Hurricanes from 151 Squadron and Spitfires from 54, 65 and 74 Squadrons, based at Hornchurch Airfield, took to the air against an unidentified enemy air attack.

The result was that Frank Rose and Pilot Officer Montague Hulton-Harrop were shot down and Hulton-Harrop was killed when his Hurricane crashed at Manor Farm, Hintlesham, Suffolk, about 5 miles west of Ipswich.

Hulton-Harrop was the first British pilot of the war shot down by a “friendly” Spitfire.

About the same time, new Type 1133 T/R VHF radios began replacing the TR9 HF sets, a new installation that allowed the wire between the antenna and the rudder to be removed.

- The first Spitfire Mk Is had numerous shortcomings.

As mentioned, the first 77s were equipped with a two-bladed wooden propeller with fixed pitch; the propeller, being fixed pitch, had to cope with the entire speed range and was therefore inefficient at take-off.

You had to roll quite a bit before you could get off the ground.

The landing gear had to be retracted or extended with a hand pump, an operation which easily caused grazed knuckles in the cramped cockpits of the Spitfires.

We took off at maximum military power, not at emergency boost pressure: we locked the throttle forward for the climb so that it could not go back, but remained stationary at that power, and we took our hand off the throttle to grab the control stick, which until then had been held in our right hand.

- At that point, you were gaining altitude; you held the control stick with your left hand, while with the other you operated the selector lever, on the right of the cockpit, until the wheels came up and the green light came on.

This required about 27 pump strokes.
The reaction to vigorous pumping was that the left hand, although holding the stick, also showed a tendency to pump, so that the aircraft showed a tendency to "porpoise" longitudinally.
From 1939 some Spitfires were disarmed and modified for photographic reconnaissance, with two cameras fitted under the wings.
Thus, after operational evaluation of these new platforms, the Photo Reconnaisance Unit (PRU) was formed in June 1940.
This unit was equipped with:

- PR-IA, for training, equipped with two F24 cameras with 127 mm lenses.
- PR-IB, with increased fuel capacity and equipped with two F24 cameras with 203 mm lenses that provided images up to a third larger. An additional 132-liter fuel tank was installed in the rear fuselage. The B type was the first to do without a bullet-resistant windshield.
- PR-IC, with a camera in the fuselage and the two wingtips moved under the left wing, with the possibility of carrying an auxiliary tank under the right (136 litres) for a total capacity of 655 litres of fuel. It was the first photographic reconnaissance aircraft to reach Kiel.
- PR-ID, of which two were built. These, unarmed, were able to carry, in addition to the onboard tanks, an additional load of 259 litres of fuel on each wing plus a load of 132 litres in the rear fuselage. The cameras, two vertically mounted F24s with 203 mm or 508 mm lenses or two vertically mounted F8s with 510 mm lenses, were located in the rear fuselage. With a full fuel load, the centre of gravity was so far aft that the aircraft was difficult to fly until the rear fuselage tank had been emptied. 230 examples were built.

On all unarmored PR conversions, the gunsight was replaced by a small camera control box from which the pilot could turn on the cameras, control the time intervals between shots, and set the number of exposures.

Spitfire Mk.II

In September 1940 the Mk.I was joined by the Mk.II, of which 972 were built, powered by the new Merlin XII engine, producing 1,150 hp at 14,000 ft (4,496 meters), on 100 octane fuel, driving a Rotol three-bladed constant speed propeller. No. 611 Squadron at Digby was the first to receive the Spitfire Mk II in August 1940.
Main features:

- Weight 2,170 - 2,800 kg
- Maximum speed 570 km/h at 5,350 meters
- Climbed to 6,096 meters in 7 minutes
- Tangency 11,460 meters.

Spitfire Mk.II

To increase the range, the long-range Mk.II was also designed, weighing 2,194-2,994 kg, whose speed was reduced, especially due to the underwing tank, to 528 km/h at 4,191 meters, with a rate of climb to 6,095 meters in 9.8 minutes, a ceiling of 8,610 meters and an additional 182-litre tank fixed under the port wing.
With this clumsy aircraft British pilots attempted to provide cover for the Blenheims on long-range missions, without much success, but there was nothing better available at the time.
These missions were named "Circus" and included, as a maximum effort, the attack on the Cologne power station,

conducted by over 50 Bristol Blenheims of which 10 were shot down, together with 4 Spitfires.
These actions continued throughout most of 1941, until the Bf-109F and FW-190 put an end to the long-range career of the Mk.II.
The Spitfire Mk.II was produced in three versions:

- Mk.IIA, which still carried the eight machine guns of the MK.I with 300 rounds each, 750 of which were produced.
- Mk.IIB, with four machine guns (300 rounds each) and two 20 mm Hispano cannon (60 rounds each), 170 built.
- Mk.IIC, maritime rescue version, 52 built, with 2 smoke bombs under the port wing, a dinghy and food parcels for the rescue of shipwrecked people, as well as additional fuel tanks. When the "C" designation was adopted to indicate the use of the C-type wing, in which any type of armament could be fitted, this variant was redesignated ASR II.

Three Squadrons operated this version, the 66th, 118th and 152nd, until it was withdrawn in March 1942.

- 66 Squadron saw some of its first combat on 10 July 1940, officially the first day of the Battle of Britain, intercepting a German reconnaissance flight and shooting down a Dornier Do 17.
- 118 Squadron was a fighter squadron that spent most of its existence flying fighters and escorting bombers over occupied Europe. No. 118 Squadron was reformed on 20 February 1941 at Filton as a fighter squadron equipped with Spitfires.
  The squadron became operational on 28 March 1941, patrolling convoys close to the British coast. This lasted until June, when the squadron began flying fighter rockets and bomber escort missions, operating over northern France. This continued throughout 1942.
  In January 1943 the squadron moved to East Anglia and began flying fighter aircraft in the Netherlands. This continued throughout the spring and summer of 1943,

until September, when the squadron moved to the north of Scotland to carry out defensive duties.

In January 1944 the squadron returned south to join the 2nd Tactical Air Force. In March it returned to Orkney and remained there for four months, not returning south until July 1944. More combat followed, mixed with bomber escort duties.

In January 1945 the squadron converted to P-51 Mustangs and on 1 February began long-range escort duties. These lasted until 3 May, and covered the period when Bomber Command returned to daylight raids. The squadron was disbanded in March 1946.

- 152nd Hyderabad Squadron was a fighter squadron that took part in the Battle of Britain, and campaigns in North Africa, Sicily and Italy, before ending the war as a fighter-bomber squadron operating in Burma.

  The squadron reformed on 1 October 1939 at Acklington and was initially equipped with the Gloster Gladiator biplane. The squadron became operational on 6 November, still using Gladiators, but they were replaced with Spitfires in January 1940. A period of defensive patrols in the north-east of England followed, before the squadron moved south to Warmwell. The squadron was based in the same area during the Battle of Britain and helped defend Portland Naval Base.

  In April 1941 the squadron moved to Cornwall to carry out convoy patrols, before moving to East Anglia in August, from where it flew bomber escort duties. In January 1942 it moved to Northern Ireland, and then in August 1942 to Pembroke, where it resumed convoy patrols for a short period.

  In late September 1942 the squadron was ordered to prepare to move overseas, to take part in Operation Torch, the Allied invasion of North Africa. Aircraft moved to Gibraltar, while the 152nd joined the invasion fleet, sailing in November. From 14 November the squadron helped provide cover for the Allied landings in Algeria, before moving to newly occupied bases in North Africa. It then followed the First Army as it moved east to

Tunisia, providing fighter defence and escort for fighter-bombers. In March 1943 the squadron became a fighter-bomber unit and performed that role for much of the remainder of the war. 152 Squadron moved to Malta in June 1943 to carry out chimney sweep operations over Sicily, then moving to Sicily shortly after the Allied landings and ashore in Italy in September.

In November 1943 the squadron began moving to India, becoming operational in Burma on 19 December. The squadron was used for defensive combat patrols, taking part in the Second Battle of Arakan in early 1944.

In April 1944 it resumed fighter-bomber operations.

The squadron operated from front line bases around Imphal during the Battle of Imphal, and supported 14th Army during the reconquest of Burma in 1945. It moved to Singapore after the Japanese surrender, and was disbanded on 10 March 1946.

Spitfire Mk.III

Following the Spitfire Mk II, the Mk III, or Type 330, was designed, of which around a thousand were to be built; however, its 1,390 hp Merlin XX engine was complex and in the end only two prototypes were completed, a modified Mk I and Mk V.
The bulletproof glass on the canopy was moved inside the cockpit, reducing drag, while the tailwheel was made retractable.

Spitfire Mk.III N3297 in March 1940, the first of two modified airframes to take the Supermarine fighter line to the next stage of development. The most obvious differences from the two earlier models are the shorter wing spanning 32 ft 7 in with clipped tips and the flaps on the landing gear doors.

The Spitfire Mk III was to be armed with four 20 mm guns, but the problem was immediate: not only was this engine sophisticated and complex, but the Hurricane, still important at the time, had to be re-engined, and would otherwise have remained hopelessly obsolete.
Thus the Merlin XX took precedence over the latter aircraft and the Spitfire Mk III never became an operational reality.
The Mk III airframe was later used to test the Merlin 61 engine, becoming the ancestor of the Spitfire Mk VII, VIII and IX.

Spitfire Mk.IV

A small number of the Spitfire Mk V, 229 of 6,479 produced, were adapted for photoreconnaissance and designated Mk IV. Two cameras were placed in the rear part of the fuselage, in a heated compartment and could take pictures on both sides of the flight path.
The pilot had a greater quantity of oxygen and the engine a greater oil reserve.

Spitfire Mk.IV

Introduced in 1941, this variant of the Spitfire was powered by the Rolls-Royce Griffon, producing 1,735 hp. Various modifications were made to accommodate this engine choice, including strengthening the fuselage and using "blister" fairings around the engine to minimise the impact on the pilot's forward visibility.
O ne of the most noticeable changes on this aircraft was the introduction of slotted flaps, supported by large hinges on the underside of the wing.

Spitfire Mk.V

In March 1941 a new version of the Spitfire, the Mark V, entered service and British Fighter Command went on the offensive.

Spitfire production, meanwhile, was rising to the point of outstripping losses.

If during the Battle of Britain 19 Spitfire Squadrons had operated, by September 1941 there were 27 and by the end of the same year as many as 46.

It was followed in production by the Mk.II and, indeed, the Spitfire Mk.V's fuselage was similar to that of the Mk.II, except for strengthened longerons, while the wing remained the same.

Powered by the 1,470 hp Rolls-Royce Merlin engine, it was divided according to two different criteria:

- The first data from the type of armament installed: Mk.VA, Mk.VB, Mk.VC.
- The second one based on the wing type:
  - LF (low flight) for the versions whose elliptical ends were truncated to obtain better aerobatic qualities and better low-altitude maneuverability.
  - HF (high flight) for aircraft intended for high-altitude interception.

The weight of the armour increased, up to 58 kg on the Spitfire Mk.VA and 69 kg on the Mk.VB.

The Mk.VA version had eight 7.7 mm Browning machine guns installed in the wings.

However, the Battle of Britain had shown that, despite their numbers, they could not match the power of the German BF-109's weapons systems, which consisted of a 20 mm cannon firing through the propeller hub, two 20 mm guns in the wings and two 7.92 mm machine guns on top of the engine cowling.

It was then decided to use a mixed armament: the Spitfire Mk.VB was, in fact, equipped with two 20 mm Hispano cannons and four 7.7 mm machine guns.

This aircraft was easily distinguishable from the others: intended to operate in desert climates, it differed from the MK.VA and the Mk.VC for the conspicuous hump under the engine, housing a complex air purification system (VOKES type sand filter) and for a new, more effective oil radiator.

- The Mk.VB was considered the workhorse of RAF Fighter Command between mid-1941 and mid-1944.

The Spitfire Mk.C, however, had the universal wing, or Type "C", first tested on the Spitfire II prototype.

- An initial configuration included the standard 7.7 mm machine guns.
- A second, 4 7.7 mm machine guns, and two 20 mm Hispano cannons.
- Finally, as a “definitive” solution for hunting large targets on the ground and in flight, four 20 mm Hispano cannons.
- In terms of air-to-ground loads, there was the option of a single 227 kg bomb or two 113 kg bombs.

The Mk.VC had its wheels moved forward by 5 centimetres and even heavier armour (87 kg), while the very latest examples were fitted with metal ailerons, which facilitated high-speed manoeuvring, ailerons, moreover, already fitted to some examples of the Mk II.
Furthermore, the Spitfire Vs were equipped with VHF radio and the carburettor problem was partly solved, but this improved engine fuel system never had characteristics comparable to the injection system adopted by the German engines.
The Spitfire Vs were powered by Merlin 45 engines, which provided an increase of 440 hp (300 kW) and 330 hp (250 kW) over the Mark I and II versions, producing 1,470 hp (9,000 ft) at 9,000 feet (2,820 meters), or Merlin 46 engines producing 1,415 hp (9,000 ft) at 14,000 feet (4,270 meters).
Both the Mk.VB and Mk.VC could carry a 500 to 800 litre drop tank under the fuselage. The empty weight, compared to the previous versions, increased from 2,180 kg to 2,300 kg and the operational weight increased from 2,620-2,675 kg to 3,070, but, thanks to the greater engine power, the speed increased ,

although only by 12 km/h, compared to that of the Mk.IA (590 km/h).
The Mk.VC Low Fighter model, in fact, reached 602 km/h at 4,000 meters.

Spitfire Mk.VB

The increased weight, however, slightly increased the climb time to 6,000 metres compared to the Mk.IIA: by 7 minutes for the previous version and by 7 minutes and 5 seconds for the Mk.VC.
Compared to the Mk.I, however, the climb time was reduced by almost two minutes.
The maximum operational ceiling rose to 11,000 meters but the range dropped from 805–925 km, still of the Mk.IIA, to 750–765 km.
Improvements such as the armoured glass, the Rotol three-bladed constant-speed propeller (227 kg versus 43 of the two-bladed wooden type), the armoured seat (33 kg in the original models), the IFF (18 kg in weight) and much more, were retained.
Additionally, the Mk.VB and C models were equipped with 20 mm Hispano Suiza cannon, albeit initially with a 60-round drum magazine, replacing four of the eight 7.7 mm Brownings.
Bomb mounts, sand filters and a carrier-borne version, the Seafire Mk.I, also soon appeared.

However, the limited amount of fuel carried by the Spitfire, which had caused little concern in the Battle of Britain, increasingly became a handicap as the aircraft was asked to fly missions deep into enemy territory.
At its optimum cruising speed of 281 miles per hour (482.4 km/h) at 10,000 feet with the engine at 2,650 rpm and the supercharger at +2 lbf pressure, a pressure which allowed the engine to compensate for the loss of power at high altitude where the air is thinner, a Mk V consumed 35 gallons (132.47 liters) of 100 octane petrol in an hour.

- In combat, with the throttle pushed full forward (full power), the engine running at 3,000 rpm in the "red zone" and with the supercharger at its maximum thrust of +16 pounds, a full tank would be emptied in little more than thirty minutes.

Of the 6,479 Spitfire Vs built in total, 94 were completed as Mk.VA, 3,932 as Mk.VB and 2,447 as Mk.VC with belt-firing guns.
On 7 March 1942, fifteen Spitfire Vs, with additional 90-gallon ventral tanks, took off from the British aircraft carrier "Eagle", off Algeria, bound for Malta, 600 miles away. These fifteen MK.Vs were the first Spitfires to see service overseas.
A further 16 arrived on the besieged island by the end of the month but, due to losses, it was decided to fly the Spitfire Vs from the Rock of Gibraltar base.
Equipped with a massive 170-gallon fuel tank, the Spitfires took more than five hours to cover the 1,100 miles separating the Rock from Malta.
By the following August, three Groups were operating on the North African front with this type of aircraft.
In early 1943, Spitfire Vs flew in defence of Darwin, Australia, and in October of the same year, three Groups (Nos. 136, 607 and 615) flying Mk.Vs began operations from Burma.

- Spitfires were increasingly used for ground attack and, from 1943, most Mk.Vs were modified by cutting off their wingtips and fitting Merlin 45 M, 50 M or 55 M engines of 1,585 hp at 850 meters, acquiring the designation LF (Low Fighter: Low altitude fighter).

With two 250 lb bombs attached under the wings, many Mk.Vs were used as bombers to attack airfields and fortifications in Sicily, releasing their bombs at 7,000 feet after an optimum 60 degree dive, after which they could compete almost on equal terms with the Fw 190, Bf 109 and the Regia Aeronautica's best fighters, the Daimler Benz-powered Macchi MC202 and MC205.

The Mk.V models were equipped with various armaments, such as the 8 x 7.7 mm machine guns but soon production began with the universal "C Wing", capable of mounting different armaments in an operational environment:

- The "A" version mounted 8 Browning machine guns with 300 rounds each.
- The "B" version 2 Hispano Suiza Mk.II cannon with 60-round drum magazine and 4 machine guns with 350 rounds.
- The "C" version could use either the "A" or "B" configuration, but in practice it mounted 2 belt-fed guns with 120 rounds and 4 machine guns with 350 rounds.

This finally improved the firing range of the guns, previously only six seconds, and made them more reliable and less cumbersome.

Normally there were only two guns, but in theory four could be mounted.

- The Seafire I carrier-based version was also a derivative of the Mk.V.

The debut took place in Algeria during Operation Torch, and on the first day the various air battles put the modest line of 36 Seafires to the test.

The first casualty was an American-built Douglas DB-7 bomber, but by the end of the day no fewer than 12 Seafires had been lost to various causes.

Missions with an aircraft still equipped with an unmodified wing , except for the very important ability to use the landing flaps, and with a rather fragile undercarriage, were overall difficult so much so that in the missions during the landing at

Salerno, in September 1943, about 40 aircraft were lost in accidents out of an initially deployed total of 126.

- The Spitfires did not arrive on Malta until March 1942.

Their presence was notable as the Hurricanes simply could not cope with the aircraft that the Italian-Germans were deploying in an attempt to crush the resistance on the island.
The first 31 Spitfires were brought to the area in March, by the aircraft carriers Argus and Eagle, which launched them from their flight decks, with extra fuel tanks to reach the island.
They were soon consumed in the very violent battle that was then raging.
The American aircraft carrier Wasp, whose intervention had been requested by Churchill since the elevators of the British carriers were not sufficient for a Spitfire without folding wings, launched another 46 on 20 April but they too did not fare any better.
Churchill then called for further intervention and on 9 May the Wasp launched another 60 aircraft, this time with experienced pilots and without the mechanical problems encountered with the previous ones.
Thus, already on May 10, the pilots of the reborn Maltese fighter boasted 14 kills against a single loss, in what was for Malta what on September 15, 1940 represented for England a historic turning point.
Since then, numerous other Spitfires reached the island with further launches, until consolidating a very respectable presence that discouraged the Italo-German aircraft from continuing the attack.
The air battles were very violent, such as those on 10 and 15 May, and then there were those in support of the Harpoon and Pedestal convoys during the summer, which managed to supply Malta with sufficient materials to continue the fight.

- The last, feeble attempt to subdue the island took place in October, but with little effort and few means.

Among the modifications of notable interest was the one which consisted of equipping the Spitfires with a gigantic fuel tank of approximately 770 litres, which allowed them to fly for over

2,000 km and thus avoid having to cross half the Mediterranean Sea for aircraft carriers, which were too exposed to the threats of the Axis.
Meanwhile, Spitfires also reached North Africa.
Despite the cumbersome Vockes filter in the nose, they proved to be capable fighters and eliminated the superiority of enemy fighters over the earlier P-40s and Hurricanes.
The Mark V provided significantly better performance than previous variants, but was still not effective enough.

- In the summer of 1941, in fact, the Luftwaffe introduced a new fighter: the Focke-Wulf Fw 190.

Spitfire Vs were among the Allied aircraft supplied to the Soviet Union under the Lend-Lease Act, but the Supermarine fighter proved to be among the most disappointing.
Not only did it not live up to its reputation, but it was often confused by VVS pilots with Messerschmitt Bf 109s and shot down.
With the Mk.V, exports of significant quantities of Spitfires to the United States finally began.
But for various reasons there was not much publicity about the British supplies of aircraft, while there was no lack of publicity when it came to American supplies to the British, even though objectively they were much more substantial.
Yet, Mosquitos and Spitfires served in the United States Army Air Forces (USAAF) and even the US Navy in significant numbers.
And so, from September 1942 the three RAF squadrons of US volunteer Spitfires became USAAF squadrons.
A specific model was the Type 353 PR Mk.IV, 229 machines built, dedicated to reconnaissance only.
Derived from the Mk.VB with Merlin 45, 46, 50, 55, 56 engines, they were the Seafire IB; 166 examples totally built from June 1942 with minimal modifications such as the arresting hook.

372 Seafire IICs were also produced on the Mk.VC basis, with 110 LF examples and the remainder standard.
Some were modified into scout aircraft.

Spitfire Mk.VI

High-altitude version with four-bladed propeller, pressurized cockpit and other improvements, such as a 1,415 hp Merlin 47 at 4,250 metres.
It was not very successful, being incapable of exceeding, in practice, 11,000 meters, and even inferior to the specially modified Mk.Vs.
The most distinctive feature of this version of the Spitfire was its extended wingtips, designed to increase its high-altitude performance.

- Ninety-seven Mk VIs were built between December 1941 and October 1942, of which 6 were sent to the Middle East, whilst the remainder remained in Britain.

A derivative version (5 built) was the PR Mk.VI high-altitude reconnaissance.

Spitfire Mk.VI

They flew some missions over Greece and were withdrawn from service in May 1943.

Spitfire Mk.VII

The Mk.VII used the closely related Merlin 61 engines with 1,300 hp at 7,010 meters (23,000 ft), Merlin 64 with 1,450 hp at 6,400 meters (21,000 ft) and Merlin 71 (16 of which were used) with 1,700 hp at 5,486 meters (18,000 ft).
The Merlin 61 was the first two-stage, two-speed supercharged engine used in the Spitfire: the two-stage supercharger improved high-altitude performance.
However, the new engines required a new cooling system, and one result was that the Mk.VII had an air intake on each wing, giving it a more symmetrical appearance than earlier Spitfires. The fuselage length was increased to 31 feet 3.5 inches in early models to accommodate the larger engine. The fuselage also had to be strengthened.

- The Mk.VII used the "C" type universal wings, capable of carrying eight machine guns, four cannon or two cannon and four machine guns depending on the situation, but with the extended wingtips used on the Mk VI.

Spitfire Mk.VII EN.474 with Merlin 64. The EN.474 was shipped to the USA, where it arrived in May 1943. This aircraft is the only surviving Spitfire VII and is currently on display at the Smithsonian National Air & Space Museum.

The Mk. VII was a pressurised fighter: it had a more advanced pressurisation system than the Mk.VI, using a sliding cockpit

canopy, more popular than the locked cockpit of the Mk.VI. The best high-altitude version of the Mk.VII was powered by the Merlin 71 and could reach 670 km/h (416 mph) at 13,411 meters (44,000 ft).
The Mk.VII remained in production, from August 1942 until early 1944, although only 140 were produced during that period. The Mk.VII was somewhat more successful than the preceding Mk.VI, but the Mk.IX proved unable to operate at high altitude, and the Mk.VII soon lost its special status as a high-altitude fighter, although it remained in use throughout the war.

Spitfire Mk.VIII

Second generation version, totally redesigned and derived, but without pressurization, from the Mk.VII.

It was built in 1,658 units, of which 160 HF, 267 F and the rest LF.

In 1941, work began to adapt the Spitfire for use of the new Merlin 61 engine.

This had a two-stage supercharger, which improved its high-altitude performance by about 50%.

The new engine was fitted to Spitfire N3297 (the only Spitfire Mk.III) and the modified aircraft first flew on 27 September 1941. The timing was perfect. September 1941 also saw the operational debut of the Fw-190.

The new German fighter outclassed the Spitfire V, then the RAF's best front-line fighter.

Tests in early 1942 proved that the Merlin 61-powered Spitfire was the answer: it reached a top speed of 666 km/h (414 mph) at 8,290 meters (27,200 ft) and could still reach 570 km/h (354 mph) at 12,200 meters (40,000 ft).

- Work thus began on redesigning the Spitfire's airframe to accommodate the new, heavier, more powerful engine.
- This work would produce the pressurised Spitfire Mk.VII and unpressurised Mk.VIII.

These aircraft were expected to be the answer to the Fw-190; if not, the interim Mk.IX would fill that role: this version used a Mk.V fuselage with as few modifications as possible and entered front-line service in July 1942, almost a year before the Mk.VIII.

- The Mk.VIII featured a strengthened fuselage with a retractable tailwheel.

Each wing carried a 53-litre (14-gallon) self-sealing fuel tank and the main fuselage fuel tank was increased in size to 363 litres (96 gallons).

Spitfire Mk.VIII

These modifications gave the Mk.VIII the same range as the Mk.V, although, because this distance was achieved at a greater speed, the Mk.VIII could remain in the air for less time than the Mk.V.

- Most Mk.VIIIs used a new broad-chord or nose rudder.

It also featured a new tropical filter, the Vokes Aero-Vee, which was so well designed that it was fitted to all Mk.VIIIs and adapted for the Mk.IX.
It used the "C" wing armament, four cannon or two cannon and two machine guns, and could carry up to 453 kg (1,000 lb) of bombs.
A Mk.VIII was the first Spitfire to use the modified cockpit seen on most later models, with a chopped-off rear fuselage and bubble canopy: this design improved visibility rearward of the aircraft and was used on the late production Mk.IXs, the very similar Mk.XVI and the late and later Mk.20s.

- In total 1,657 Mk.VIIIs were produced, so although it never replaced the Mx.IX in Britain and Northern Europe, it was, nevertheless, a mainstay version of the Spitfire.

It was produced in three versions.

- The F.VIII, which used the 1,560 hp Merlin 61, was the standard fighter model.
- The HF.VIII which used a 1,655 hp Merlin 70 and was a high-altitude fighter.
- The LF.VIII which used the 1,705 hp Merlin 66 and was officially a low-altitude fighter, although its best altitude was not much lower than that of the F model.

The success of the Mk.IX reduced the importance of the Mk.VIII. Although the first production model was completed in November 1942, it took until June 1943 for the first squadron to be equipped with it. One reason for the delay was that it had been decided to use the Mk.VIII in the Mediterranean and Far East, and so the first squadron to use it was No. 145 Squadron, based at Malta.

By the summer of 1943 the crisis in the Mediterranean was over and the Mk.VIII saw most of its service during the invasion of Italy, often in a ground attack role.

The Mk.VIII arrived in the Far East towards the end of 1943.

It was just in time, because in early 1944 the Japanese launched their Arakan Offensive.

The Mk.V had been on a par with the best Japanese fighter in Burma, the Ki 44 "Tojo", but the Mk.VIII was much faster and, indeed, the Japanese Air Force was soon driven from the skies over the Arakan, allowing the Allies to resupply their isolated troops from the air.

The same pattern was repeated in March 1944 when Allied air forces in India managed to maintain supplies for 55,000 troops at Kohima and Imphal.

Finally, the Mk.VIII was used by the Royal Australian Air Force, initially for the defence of Darwin, but when the Japanese were pushed back it was used more often for ground attacks, keeping isolated Japanese garrisons under control.

Spitfire Mk.IX

After a long and painful period in which the British lost four fighters for every opponent shot down, to counter the last formidable German fighters (Bf 109F-4 and G included) the Mk.IX model was developed which once again represented a milestone and of which more than 5,500 examples were produced.
It entered service in July 1942, proving superior in tests against captured Focke-Wulf 190s, and was produced until the end of the war.

Spitfire Mk.IX

The Spitfire Mk.VIII was supposed to be the definitive one, but this never was, because the development of this redesigned model, a bit like the Macchi MC205N, took too long and proved complex.
The re-engineering of the Spitfire Mk.V with the Rolls-Royce Merlin 61 with two-stage supercharger, in place of the Merlin 45, was a great improvement.

- The nominal power went from about 1,440 to 1,660 hp, and if above 6-7 thousand meters the Spitfire became progressively lazier and more inert to the controls, due to a lack of power, at 9,000 meters, the new engine still allowed 1,000 hp, a good double of the previous one.

The Spit Mk.IX, still reasonably light and very agile, seemed to climb higher and higher as one approached the straphosphere: one could fly in formation at 13,000 meters, out of reach of all German fighters, including the deadly FW-190s.
It was not a useful action, since from there nothing could be done except to give the German defences a certain level of psychological humiliation, possibly by luring the fighters to altitudes where they would have the worst of it against the new Spitfires.

- The climb had also improved. In fact, it was becoming a strength never seen before.

The climb time to 6,100 meters was normally given as about 5.8 minutes, in reality, climbing with the engine at full throttle, this would normally have been possible for no more than 5 minutes, and with the radiators closed, climb times of just 4.5-4.85 minutes were recorded.
Not only that, but the time to about 8,000 meters was less than 7 minutes, and 9,000 (30,000 feet) was reached in just 9-10 minutes, although then even the Spitfire was beginning to feel the lack of oxygen.

- With these times, 1 or 2 minutes better than those of the Italian “5” series fighters and slightly better than those of the Bf-109G-1, the Spitfire was truly a formidable interceptor.

The climb under normal power and with external loads was on the order of 5.5 minutes or about 6.5 with a 227 kg bomb.
The Macchi MC205, probably the best of the Italian medium-low altitude interceptor fighters, reached 6,000 meters in 5 minutes and 53 seconds, 7 minutes with the engine at normal power.

In a dive it was less efficient, but the carburetor was modified and allowed it to be less affected by negative acceleration.
Most Mk.IXs of all types used the standard “C” wing, which could carry four 20 mm cannon or two 20 mm cannon and four 7.7 mm (.303 in) machine guns.
From 1944 some were built with the “E” wing, which replaced the four 7.7 mm machine guns with two 12.7 mm (.50 in) heavy machine guns with 250 rounds each, along with two Hisso cannon with 120 rounds each.
Handling and climb were excellent for both the Italian fighters and the Spitfire, so in the event of a collision the difference between the two was the skill of the pilot and any initial advantage he had.

- The Spitfire IX could fly up to 13,000 meters, compared to 11,000 meters previously.
- The difference with the Mk.V was especially marked at high altitude, while in absolute terms the top speed rose to over 650 km/h.

With what was virtually the same engine, the P-51 Mustang was capable of over 700 km/h despite a much greater weight, but the climb, handling, firepower and ceiling of the lighter Spitfire Mk.IX were superior, with the ability to climb to 30,000 feet in less than 8-10 minutes versus around 13 minutes for the P-51.

There were 3 main versions of the Mk.IX.

- The standard F.IX used the Merlin 61, and was the only version produced until early 1943: 1,255 F.Mk IXs were produced.
- It was later joined by a version powered by the Merlin 66, which featured a new fuel injection carburettor in place of the float carburettor of earlier models, completely solving the fuel flow problems during zero-gravity manoeuvres and inverted flight. This engine gave its best performance at slightly lower altitudes than the Merlin 61. Spitfires fitted with this engine were designated LF.Mk.IX: this was the most numerous version of the Mk.IX, with 4,010 produced.

- Eventually , 410 high-altitude HF.Mk.IXs were produced using the Merlin 70 engine, with improved high-altitude performance.

The Mk.IX was certainly a very successful aircraft, and literally put the Mk.VIII in the shade.
This entered production around 1943 and was produced in approximately 1,700 examples while the Mk.IX was put into service already in 1942, immediately obtaining a positive response against the Bf-109G and, above all, against the feared Fw 190.
The Fw 190 was never an easy target for anyone, and below 6,000 metres it was still competitive with the Mk.IX, but above that the difference in power gave the British machine a greater advantage.
A reconnaissance model, derived from the Mk.IX, was a natural evolution.
A few other Spitfires had already been fitted out for this task, but the Mk.XI proved to be the best.
Equipped only with cameras, auxiliary tanks behind the cockpit for a total of about 900 litres, it had a long range and excellent speed performance, being capable of about 675 km/h while in a dive it reached over 960 km/h.
His operational record was of the utmost importance to the RAF, performing unescorted flights as far as Germany.

Spitfire Mk.X

The pressurised PR Mk.X entered service in 1944, due to its low priority status: only 16 were produced.
The PR.X featured the pressurised cabin features of the Spitfire Mk.VII but was, in practice, similar to the PR.XI.
The PR.X was not much appreciated by pilots and was only operational with two squadrons for a short period of just over a year: furthermore, it was realised that pressurisation was not necessary for most reconnaissance missions.

Spitfire PR Mk.X fitted with pressurised cockpit.

Furthermore, the PR.X's thick canopy reduced visibility, a crucial factor for reconnaissance missions.
The increased complexity of maintaining the pressurized cabin systems also proved to be a disadvantage.
The Spitfire PR.XI and PR.X played an essential role in aerial reconnaissance during the Second World War.
The PR.XI, with its versatility and robust performance, became the predominant PR variant, while the PR.X, despite its advanced pressurisation system, was less favoured due to

operational inefficiencies and limited need for high-altitude reconnaissance.

These aircraft demonstrated the adaptability of the Spitfire platform to meet a variety of mission requirements, contributing significantly to Allied intelligence gathering efforts.

Spitfire Mk.XI

The Mk.XI was essentially a Spitfire Mk.IX interceptor modified for photo-reconnaissance with cameras, a more powerful engine and a larger oil tank in the nose.
All guns and armor were removed and fuel capacity was greatly increased: speed was the defense of the unarmed Mark XI.

- A total of 471 Mk.XIs were built between April 1943 and January 1946: they were powered by Merlin 61, 62, 63A and 70 engines, the latter producing 1,655 hp.

Britain and its allies flew various photo-reconnaissance versions of the Spitfire with great success in all theatres during the Second World War.
The 14th Photographic Squadron of the United States Army Air Forces 8th Air Force operated Spitfire Mk.XIs from November 1943 to April 1945, flying dangerous long-range reconnaissance missions over continental Europe. Displayed in 1993, this aircraft is painted as a 14th Photographic Squadron Mk.XI at Mount Farm Airfield in England.
The Mk.XI was the first PR variant to have the option of using two vertically mounted F52 cameras with 36-inch focal length lenses in the fuselage aft of the cockpit. Several other configurations could be fitted, depending on mission requirements; the X Type installation, for example, had two vertically mounted F24s with 14-inch lenses and one obliquely mounted F24 with an 8-inch lens mounted on top and facing to port.

- The PR Mk.XIs used for tactical reconnaissance had an additional vertically oriented camera in a fairing under each wing.

The Mk.XIs had a deeper front fairing to accommodate a larger 55 litre (14.5 gal) oil tank and used the unarmored wrap-around PRU windscreen.
The booster pumps for the wing tanks were mounted and covered by teardrop-shaped fairings under the wings.

Retractable tailwheels were fitted as standard.
260 Mk.XIs were powered by Merlin 61, 63 or 63A engines, with the remaining 211 using the high-altitude Merlin 70: all Merlin 70s and 198 Merlin 60 series aircraft were fitted with the Vokes Aero-Vee dust filter in the carburettor air intake.

Spitfire Mk.XI

All Merlin 60-powered aircraft featured the fuel radiator in the left leading edge wing root.

- Additional quick-detachable tanks could be fitted under the centre section; in common with the Mk.IX, these could have a capacity of 113, 170 or 340 litres (30, 45 or 90 gallons) and, for the Mk.XI, a 643-litre (170 gallon) tank was also available.

The Spitfire Mk.XIs were capable of a maximum speed of 417 mph (671 km/h) at 24,000 feet (7,300 meters) and could travel at 395 mph (636 km/h) at 32,000 feet (9,800 meters).
Normally, Spitfire XIs flew between these altitudes, although in an emergency the aircraft could climb to 44,000 feet (13,000

meters): however, the pilots could not survive at such altitudes for long in an unpressurised cockpit without suffering serious physiological effects.
Initially, production of the Mk.XI was delayed because development of the Mk.VII and VIII series was delayed. As a result, it was decided to base the Merlin 60-powered aircraft on the MK.IX airframe.
The first Mk.XIs were built in November 1942: from April 1944 production continued concurrently with the PR Mk.XIX before ending in December 1944, when they were gradually phased out in favour of the Mk.XIX.

Spitfire Mk.XII

The prototype was based on a Mk.II airframe.
The Merlin engine was replaced with a Griffon II with a single-stage, two-speed supercharger, developing 1,735 hp: the airframe needed to be strengthened to cope with the increased power and torque of the new engine.
The first Griffon-engined Spitfires made their operational debut in early 1943.
They were designated Mk.XII and had been developed from the experimental Mk.IV model, which flew in late 1941.

Spitfire Mk.XII MB.882 of the 41st Squadron.

The aircraft was designed to be a high-performance low-altitude fighter and was delivered with clipped wings to improve maneuverability.
The main difference between the Griffon and the Merlin, apart from the increase in displacement from 27.2 litres to 36 litres, was that the Griffon engine required a large diameter (over 3 meters) 4-bladed propeller and turned to the right rather than the left, leaving the aircraft nose-heavy, which incidentally had a lower propeller position than the “high nose” of the Merlin; but once in the air it was a formidable aircraft.
Below 6,000 meters it was perhaps the fastest of the world's fighters, but its 322-liter (85 gallon) fuel tank left it only 620 km of range.

- Among its innovations, the rivets with drowned heads to minimize aerodynamic resistance.

Compared to the Spitfire Mk.V, the bulge above the gun feed on the main deck was much smaller, the rudder and trim tabs were larger, and the engine cowlings and nose cone differed significantly to accommodate the Griffon engine.
The universal wing of the Spitfire Mk.V was fitted: armament consisted of two 20 mm cannon and four 7.7 mm (.303 in) machine guns.
While early models were based on the Spitfire Mk.V airframe, later aircraft used the Spitfire Mk.VIII fuselage, incorporating refinements such as flush riveting and a retractable tailwheel.
Fuel capacity was 322 litres (85 gallons), while operating weight with full fuel and ammunition was 3,356 kg (7,400 lb).

- The resulting aircraft was very fast at low altitude, reaching a speed of 599 km/h (372 mph) at 1,750 meters (5,700 ft) and 640 km/h (397 mph) at 5,485 meters (18,000 ft).

It was, therefore, faster than the Mk.IX up to about 6,100 meters (20,000 ft), but beyond that height it was slower.
Below 20,000 feet, thanks also to its truncated wings, it was about 14 mph faster than the Mk.IX.
It was apparently a little nose heavy, but it was fun to fly, and in agility it even surpassed the earlier types with the Merlin.

- At low altitude it left the FW-190 and Typhoon behind, and still had superior agility.

He was the protagonist of the hunt for V-1 missiles, and it's a shame that they produced so few of them.
The Spitfire Mk.XII was not very successful as a land machine, while the Seafire Mk.XV was the naval derivative with a 1,850 hp Griffon VI engine and four-bladed propeller.
It was a late production machine, with 256 built by Westland Aircraft and 134 by Owen.
The Mk XII was strictly an interim design and for once (unlike the Mk.V and Mk.IX) did not enter mass production.

Only 100 were built, equipping two squadrons: No. 41 received its Mk XIIs in February 1943 and No. 91 in April 1943.
The low-altitude performance of the Mk.XII was, however, very useful when dealing with low-level hit-and-run raids mounted by the Fw 190 and later helped against the V-1. However, it was not until the Mk.XIV that the Griffon-engined Spitfires demonstrated their potential.

Spitfire Mk.XIII

The PR Mk.XIII was the last Spitfire photo-reconnaissance variant based on the Mk.V. airframe: designed specifically for low-altitude reconnaissance, it was equipped with two vertical and one obliquely mounted cameras.
Due to the greater risks posed by low-level flight, the PR Mk.XIII was one of the few reconnaissance variants that retained an armament of four 7.7 mm machine guns, providing some degree of self-defence.

Supermarine Spitfire PR Mk.XIII.

It was equipped with the Merlin 32 engine and a three-bladed DH propeller.
The aircraft was also equipped with a bulletproof windshield and the PR-style sliding canopy.
The PR Mk XIII's fuel capacity was similar to that of the standard fighter version, which somewhat limited its range: however, it played a vital role in photographing the Normandy beaches in the run-up to the D-Day invasion.
18 were built.

Spitfire Mk.XIV

The first important Griffon-powered Spitfire was the Mk XIV, which finally broke out of low altitude thanks to the development of the RR Griffon with twin-stage supercharging, the Griffon 61, a two-speed, two-stage supercharger, providing 2,050 hp.

It was installed on the basic Mk.VIII airframe, suitably modified, “E” wing, with the 5-bladed propeller needed for the 2,050 hp available: in essence, the rule was to use one blade for, at most, 400 hp.

Early models used the universal “C” type wing with 4 x 20 mm cannon or 2 x 20 mm cannon and four 7.7 mm machine guns, while later production used the “E” wing with 2 x 12.7 mm machine guns instead of the 7.7 mm.

The fuselage was lengthened by 36 cm and looked even more robust than its predecessors: the Griffons gave the Spitfires a much more massive nose, almost more than the rear part of the fuselage.

- 957 were produced, 430 of which were used as the FR Mk.XIVE reconnaissance fighter, featuring the F-24 camera and teardrop cockpit, which allowed for a wider vertical rudder chord.

They normally had 498 litres of fuel, but additional fuel tanks could be added outside and inside.

Initially, six Mk.VIIIs were converted, which entered service on 20 January 1943, demonstrating in this guise a rate of climb of 1,500 metres per minute, and over 720 km/h at 7,600 meters, a spectacular performance.

However, it was now difficult to control, with all that excess power.

- There was an increase in tail area and a three-bladed contra-rotating propeller was also tested, later applied in similar form to the Seafire 46 and 47.

It was not until January 1944 that they were put into service with No.610 Squadron, immediately proving to be a "hot plane": around 718 km/h, climbing to 6,100 meters (20,000 feet) in around 5 minutes: the only problem was a certain lateral instability and a slightly shorter range given the fuel consumption, despite the 415 litres (109.5 gallons), with around 760 km of autonomy.
It was not a fighter without its flaws and many pilots preferred, in terms of handling and flight capabilities, the Mk.V, perhaps the best in terms of handling.

- But that was what progressive development required, adding ever greater performance.

The restored Spitfire Mk.XIV RM927, flying in October 2023.

As when it came to shooting down the V-1s, which, thanks to the 150 octane fuel, became coveted prey: over 640 km/h, or about 50 km/h more than normal, thanks to the thrust of 11.3 kg (25 lbs), at an altitude of 610 meters.
They were not widely used, however, with only 6 squadrons in service in Northern Europe in December 1944.

- Adolf Galland commented on this: The best thing about the Mk.XIVs was that there were very few of them!

The Mk.XIV was so powerful, that it could climb almost at full throttle without losing speed, at a rate of 1,500 meters per minute (5,000 ft/min).
Gradually the aircraft were equipped with clipped wings, and faced savagely against the FW-190D and Bf-109G and K.
They will only arrive in the Far East in June 1945, by then too late to challenge the Japanese.
Despite the increase in weight and power, the Spitfire remained relatively lightly wing-loaded and still retained good handling for an aircraft that could now pull around 200 kg/m ^{2}, not unlike the Bf-109.

- The armament of two 20 mm cannon and two 12.7 mm machine guns became more effective with newer fire control systems such as the K-14, while the Bf-109G and K relied on a single Mk 108 cannon which, although it had an effective range of around 300 meters, was still capable of splitting a Spitfire in two with a single hit.

Added to this was the Flak, and of course, the FW-190s, never easy opponents.
The Spitfire was more agile and more or less as fast as something better armed; the use of very high octane fuel allowed superpower that did not need systems like the German MW50 water-methanol, which was certainly a good thing also for the life of the engine and spark plugs: furthermore; the dive, with the Griffon, was no longer affected by power losses with negative G.
Here is the assessment of the Mk.XIV, described as a Mk.VIII with a Griffon engine and 5-bladed Rotol propeller, rather than the Merlin and 4-bladed propeller.
At around 3,800 kg, total without external loads, its wing loading was indeed much higher than the approximately 150 kg/m^2 of the Spitfire Mk.VIII and IX, and not that different from the Bf-109G and K, especially when truncated wings and ever-increasing external loads were later adopted.
The climb was over 1,500 meters per minute at about 500 meters, and over 1,000 meters per minute at over 6,000 meters.
The climb was, despite the weight, such that the following could be achieved (with the radiators open):

- 2' and 18 seconds for the 3,050 meters
- 5' and 6 seconds for 6,096 meters
- 6' and 50 seconds for about 8,000 meters
- 8' 21 seconds for 9,150 meters
- Approximately 15' for 12,200 meters

This of course was with the maximum combat overpressure, at 2,750 rpm and +18 lbs, while at about 3,600 kg the speed was about 580 km/h, 718 km/h at about 7,600 meters.

As for climb times, although not easy to compare, it is worth remembering that they exceeded the best available on the RE.2005 by 30 seconds, and about 1 minute at 8,000 meters; over 2 minutes vs the MC205V, more than the various G.55, C.205N.

The G.55, at 3,680 kg, took 7.2 minutes to 6,000 meters, roughly the performance of a typical Spitfire Mk.V, and over 10 minutes to 8,000 meters.

Even the more similar G.56 was still able to climb to 7,000 meters in 7.1 minutes, while the Spitfire Mk.XIV took 6.2 minutes to reach 7,300 meters.

These were the performances at “combat rating”, but in climb at normal power the Spitfire was not so extraordinary, limiting itself to climbing at lower speeds, of the order of 7 minutes to 6,100 meters.

Subsequently many Spitfires of this type were exported, for example 70 to India and 132 to Belgium.

The Mk.XIV's superior performance made it the ideal aircraft to deal with the V-1 threat: 91 Squadron, based at West Malling, achieved the best result against the flying bombs, shooting down 184 with its Mk.XIVs.

Spitfire Mk.XV

The Supermarine Seafire was a naval version of the Supermarine Spitfire specially adapted for operation from aircraft carriers: the Seafire's mission was primarily as a short-range interceptor.
The Mk.XV variant of the Seafire was powered by a Griffon VI, single-stage supercharger, rated at 1,850 hp driving a 3.17 meters (10 ft 5 in) Rotol propeller, giving a speed of 578 km/h (359 mph).

Spitfire Mk.XV Seafire.

It looked like a naval Spitfire Mk.XII, but was an amalgamation of a strengthened Seafire III airframe and wings with wingtip fuel tanks, retractable tailwheel, larger elevators and wide-chord 'pointed' rudder from the Spitfire Mk.III.
The engine cowling was of the Spitfire Mk.II series, secured with more fasteners and lacking the acorn-shaped bubble behind the spinner.

- A V-shaped guard in front of the tail wheel prevented the arresting cables from becoming tangled in the tail wheel.

A problem that immediately emerged was the poor behaviour of this model, especially on take-off: at full power, in fact, the propeller wake, which oscillated to the left, unlike the Merlin, which oscillated to the right, often forced the Seafire to turn to starboard, even with the rudder in the completely opposite position.
The hydraulic undercarriage legs were still the same as those of the Merlin-engined Spitfires, which meant that turning was often accompanied by a series of jumps: this undercarriage also gave it a tendency for the propeller tips to 'peck' the deck on landing and occasionally bounce off the arresting cables.

Spitfire Mk.XVI

Similar version to the Mk.IX, but with an engine built by the American Packard, in a specific model called Merlin 266 with 1,752 hp with modified carburettor and a speed of 645 km/h
The early Mk.XVIs were equipped with a truncated "C" type wing with four 20 mm cannon or two 20 mm cannon and four 7.7 mm machine guns, plus 450 kg of bombs; later "E" type wing with two 12.7 mm machine guns instead of four 7.7 mm: cockpit with bubble canopy.

Spitfire Mk.XVI

Most of the Mk.XVIs produced had clipped wings, which improved their roll rate.

- It was produced in 1,066 units starting from 1944 and remained in production until 1945.

It was used as a fighter-bomber against V2 missile sites and airfields in the final months of the European war and a handful remained in RAF service until the mid-1950s.

Spitfire Mk.XVII

The Seafire XVII was the first of the Seafire variants to feature a shortened rear fuselage and distinctive teardrop canopy. The aircraft could carry a heavier weapons load due to its strengthened construction, with fuel and rocket tanks under the wings.

Produced from the Seafire XV, this aircraft flew on the front line until the early 1950s, when it was downgraded to training duties.

It operated effortlessly from aircraft carriers, making it a formidable presence on land and sea: its folding wings allowed it to take off rapidly and land on the decks of naval vessels, extending its range and influence across the ocean.

The impressive design ensured agility and speed, boasting sleek, aerodynamic contours that radiated elegance and increased maneuverability.

It reached top speeds of about 378 miles per hour (608 km/h).

A Spitfire Mk.XVII Seafire with Griffon engine and folded wings.

S pitfire Mk.XVIII

The Spitfire Mk.XVIII was a later model, derived from the previous one, with additional fuel and a strengthened structure; it did not reach wartime service and only a few were produced by 1946: 18 were sent to India in 1947, of the 300 newly assembled.

Structurally it was a Mk.XIV with strengthened landing gear and structure, practically at the end of the war: it had a bubble canopy and a chopped fuselage.

It was armed with the "E" wing, with two 20 mm cannons and two machine guns. 12.7mm Browning M2, or four 20mm guns.

Spitfire Mk.XVIII

300 were produced, 100 in fighter configuration, while 200 were FR (Fighter Reconnaissance) aircraft, which sacrificed some fuel capacity to carry two F.24 vertical cameras and one F.24 oblique camera.

It used either a 2,035 hp Griffon 65 or a 2,340 hp Griffon 67.

The Mk XVIII saw service after the Second World War, in Malaya and Palestine.

S- pitfire Mk.XIX

The final reconnaissance aircraft was the PR Mk.XIX, essentially a Mk.XI with the Mk.XIV's Griffon engine, and soon also had a pressurised cockpit.
It was produced by combining the Mk.XIV fuselage, the PR Mk.XI wings and the PR.Mk X cabin.
All but the first 22 of the 225 produced had a pressurized cockpit.

Spitfire PR Mk.XIX

It could carry up to 961 litres (254 US gallons) of fuel internally, using space in the wings that originally housed the cameras. It could also carry a 643 litre (170 US gallon) drop tank, although the largest size used for operations was 340 litres (90 US gallons).
It had a top speed of 716 km/h (445 mph) and a service ceiling of 13,000 meters (42,600 ft), making it almost impossible for the Luftwaffe to capture.

- The Pr Mk.XIX could carry two vertical cameras and one oblique camera on the port side: the vertical cameras were either an F.8 with a focal length of 14 or 20 inches or an F.52 with a focal length of 20 inches. The oblique camera was an F.24 with a focal length of 8 or 14 inches.

The Pr Mk.XIX first flew in April 1944 and entered service in May 1944.

The last operational flight of an RAF Spitfire was made by a PR Mk.IX on 1 April 1954.

Three continued to fly with the Temperature and Humidity Flight, performing meteorological research, until they were finally retired on June 10, 1957.

On 5 February 1952 a Spitfire Mk.XIX of No. 81 Squadron RAF based in Hong Kong reached probably the highest altitude ever achieved by a Spitfire.

The pilot, Flight Lieutenant Ted Powles, was on a routine flight to take outside air temperatures and report on other weather conditions at various altitudes in preparation for a proposed new air service through the area.

It climbed to 50,000 feet (15,240 meter) indicated altitude, with an actual altitude of 51,550 feet (15,712 meters), which was the highest altitude ever recorded for a Spitfire.

However, cabin pressure dropped below a safe level and, in an attempt to reduce altitude, he entered an uncontrollable dive that shook the aircraft violently: he eventually regained control below 3,000 feet (900 meters), managing to land without any obvious damage to his aircraft.

Evaluation of recorded flight data suggested that in the dive it reached a speed of 690 mph (1,110 km/h) or Mach 0.91, which would have been the highest speed ever achieved by a propeller-driven aircraft: it is now generally believed that this speed figure is the result of inherent instrument errors and should be regarded as unrealistic.

Spitfire Mk.21

With the Mk.21, the Spitfire marking classification changed from Roman to Arabic numerals.
This was perhaps the first Spitfire criticised for going a little too far beyond the limits of the design.
There were several development problems, ailerons with a critical supersonic control reversal speed and a wing with a 47% greater stiffness than other versions.
Armament consisted of four 20 mm guns, this time with 150 rounds each.

Spitfire Mk. 21 of the 91st Squadron

Ultimately the Mk.21, which only entered full service after the war, was a more difficult machine to handle, nose heavy, a bit like putting a three-litre engine in a small car, but in climbs and dives it was superior to the Spitfire Mk.IX.

- A formidable aircraft, even against the best FW-190 it would have had no problems.

The usual engine was a Griffon 61 or 64 with a five-bladed propeller, although some were fitted with the Griffon 85 with six blades in two sets of three rotating in different directions, known as a contra-rotating propeller, to make full use of the Griffon's 2,375 hp.

However, the large, powerful Griffons fitted to the later Spitfires made manoeuvring the aircraft difficult on the ground.

- Version ordered in 1,500 units; but only 12 were completed, and a third of them were even used only as gun targets.

No. 91 Squadron saw its first service in January 1945, but they did not see long combat, although they did have some successes, for example when they sank a German mini-submarine on 26 April.
From the Mk.21 project 50 Seafire Mk.45 were derived.

Spitfire Mk.22

The Mk.22 was a development of the Mk.21: it used the shortened fuselage and bubble canopy seen on most other late Spitfires, but this reintroduced the instability seen in the Mk.21. The response was to install a much larger tail, increasing the control services area by more than 25%: production began in March 1945, but the aircraft did not arrive in time to see active service in the Pacific.

- The RAF initially ordered 627 of the aircraft, however, the end of the war reduced this number to 260: 20 Spitfires were sold to Egypt, 11 to Rhodesia and 10 to Syria.

Spitfire Mk.22

To avoid yawing on take-off, some had two three-bladed counter-rotating propellers, which were heavy but capable of cancelling out the yawing moment.
From the Mk.22 project 24 Seafire Mk.46.1 were derived

Spitfire Mk.24

The Mk.23, which had a different type of wing, having failed, the final version was the Mk.24, which was similar to the 22 but with more fuel capacity.

The Spitfire Mk.24 was the last production model of the famous Supermarine Spitfire: a total of 54 Mk.24s were produced, in addition to 27 examples rebuilt from previous Mk.22 models: 16 examples were sent to Hong Kong, while 24 were stored without even being used by the units.

The Mk.24 was largely similar to the preceding Mk.22, with the exception of having two fuel tanks in the rear fuselage installed and different rocket mounts which allowed the installation of up to eight RP-3 rockets compared to the six of the Mk.22.

The main armament was also different, as some later production Mk.24s were armed with four shorter, lighter, electrically operated 20 mm Hispano Mk.V cannon with 650 rounds in total.

- The engine was a Griffon 61 or 64 of 2,050 hp and 2,375 hp respectively, driving an 11 ft diameter 5-bladed Rotol propeller.

With the second engine, maximum speed was 628 km/h (390 mph) at sea level, 730 km/h (454 mph) at 5,800 meters (19,000 ft); rate of climb was 1,550 meters/min (5,100 ft/min) at sea level.

Some examples were fitted with the Griffon 85 driving a 6-bladed contra-rotating propeller, although, unlike earlier Mk.21s so fitted, none appear to have seen operational use.

The Mk 24 also possessed increased engine power due to the use of 150 octane fuel, which was not available on the preceding Mk.22.

But by now the Spitfire had been superseded by jets such as the Vampire and Meteor, and the RAF was faced with post-war cutbacks and a near-collapse national economy.

The last Spitfire Mk. 24 remained in service in Hong Kong until 1955.

This gives an idea of the complexity of Spitfire production, over 22,000 of which were built despite the destruction of Supermarine's main factories by LW in September 1940.
Only the dispersion in numerous secondary factories managed to save the Spitfire from extinction due to “natural causes”.

Spitfire Mk.24

This latest variant of the Spitfire was among the finest piston-engined fighters of all time, capable of operating effectively in a wide variety of roles, and might have been built in far greater numbers and seen more widespread service had the jet age not arrived so early.
Derived from the Mk.24 were the Seafire Mk.47.

Use

The Spitfire found several fighters in the Italian skies that proved to be worthy adversaries.
The Macchi MC202 Folgore, in particular, was almost on par with the Spitfire Mk.V: equally fast, it outperformed it in turns, but was less armed and had a slower rate of climb.
The Macchi MC205, in 1943, in addition to maintaining the greater maneuverability, closed the gap in armament and detached the Mk.V in climb rate, configuring itself as a very respectable opponent of the Spitfire V.

"In general the standard of flying of the Italian pilots was very high ," writes Scottish ace Grp. Capt Wilfrid Duncan Smith (19 kills) in his book "Spitfire into battle," " *and in battles with the Macchi 205s in particular we were up against aircraft that could turn and duel with our Spitfires extremely well."*

Duncan Smith himself, a friend of the other great British ace, Douglas Bader, and father of the Conservative Party leader of the same name, had tested himself with another Series 5 fighter, the Reggiane Re.2005, and was even more impressed by it.

«Having clashed in a dogfight with a Reggiane 2005», he also says in "Spitfire into battle", *«I am convinced that it would have been very difficult for us to win, with our Spitfires, if the Italians or Germans had had some squadron equipped with these aircraft at the beginning of the Sicilian campaign or in operations from Malta. Fast, and with excellent maneuverability, the Reggiane 2005 was overall a superb airplane. (...) Neither the Macchi 205, nor the Messerschmitt 109G could match the Reggiane 2005 in maneuverability and rate of climb. I think it was the best aircraft produced by Italy in the Second World War».*

But even the Reggiane Re.2001, although slower and less armed, could give the Spitfire Mk.V a hard time in manoeuvred

combat, as the British ace Laddie Lucas recalls in his "Malta: The thorn in Rommel's side".
On 13 July 1942, over Malta, Jack Rae, then on the verge of becoming one of New Zealand's most gifted pilots, and his able number 2, Alan Yates, of 249 Squadron, spotted a Reggiane that was about to leave the fight and return to base.
What followed gave Rae such a shock that it remained vividly etched in his memory for half a century.

"I had never been involved in such a complex series of aerobatics before, while chasing him. On two occasions I almost went into a spin following his manoeuvres. I found it difficult to get an advantageous position to open fire, while the Italian pilot, on several occasions, came dangerously close to hitting me.
Eventually his engine started smoking and I knew I had damaged his tail.
However, finding ourselves in the middle of the Strait of Sicily, with little fuel and little ammunition, we decided to reverse course, so as not to risk finding ourselves in difficulty if attacked in turn.
But as we turned back to base, leaving our opponent smoking profusely, to my amazement I saw that he had also turned. He made one last attack, in defiance, just to show what he thought of a pair of Spitfires."

Spitfires also flew with the Soviet Air Force's red star.
In November 1941, the RAF sent three PR Mk.IV reconnaissance aircraft to Vaenga in northern Russia to monitor the movements of German warships.
The personnel of the Soviet Air Force (VVS) were favorably impressed by the characteristics of the Supermarine reconnaissance aircraft.
Thus, in early October 1942, Joseph V. Stalin wrote to Winston Churchill, requesting the urgent delivery of a good number of Spitfires.
Churchill agreed to send an initial consignment of 150 aircraft, with spare parts, equivalent to another 50 aircraft.
Deliveries of the Spitfire Mk.VBs began in the spring of 1943.

These were the first Supermarine fighters officially exported.

- In May 1943, 143 Mk.VBs were sent to Russia, and from then until the fall of Berlin, approximately 1,200 more followed.

But the Soviet pilots were not particularly satisfied with the Supermarine fighter, highlighting its structural defects, even serious ones, common to most versions: the landing gear, for example, with its narrow track, was not suited to grassy or uneven runways.

The close spacing between the landing gear legs meant that the aircraft tended to swing dangerously when taxiing on uneven ground, with the risk of a wingtip touching the ground.

- Also, like the Hurricane, the centre of mass was positioned towards the front, so the Spitfire could easily tip forward and hit the runway with its propeller blades or become nose-down.

For this reason, the flight manual expressly prohibited taxiing on soft ground without a man sitting astride the tail to balance its weight.

In the Pacific the Spitfire found a formidable opponent in the Mitsubishi A6M Zero: light, sleek and exceptionally maneuverable, this long-range fighter served with the Imperial Japanese Navy throughout the war in the Far East, from the attack on Pearl Harbor until the last desperate sorties against B-29 bombers in August 1945.

Spitfires first clashed with the Japanese on Boxing Day, 1943.

A pair of Spitfires attacked a large formation of Japanese fighter aircraft over Chittagong, shooting down four fighters and bombers.

On the last day of 1943, Royal Australian Air Force (RAAF) Spitfire pilots shot down 11 Japanese bombers and 3 fighters, earning a commendation from Winston Churchill.

In the air battles over Chittagong in 1943-44, Spitfires achieved numerous successes against Japanese bombers.

Spitfire losses, however, became alarmingly high when they ventured into open sea, as the RAAF discovered during the defence of Darwin, due to the limited range of the British fighters, which not infrequently ran out of fuel and were unable to return.

- And the Zeros proved superior in maneuverable combat.

"The famous Spitfire, recalled the American Flying Tiger ace Gregory "Pappy" Boyington in his book Baa Baa Black Sheep, was no match for the Japanese Zero. They came back full of holes after clashes with the fighters of the Rising Sun."

In close combat, the Japanese fighter could easily outmaneuver Mitchell's fighter.
Spitfire Mk.VIII pilots operating over Burma learned in battle with Mitsubishi fighters that if they followed the rules adopted by the Flying Tigers with their famous shark-mouthed P-40s, no low-level, low-speed dogfights, they had little to fear.

- Otherwise they were inexorably destroyed.

Fighting the Japanese proved to be a particularly challenging task.
Several RAF Squadrons were deployed to Australia in 1943.
Although British fighters were reported to have achieved success against the fast Ki-46 reconnaissance aircraft, claiming 18 kills in total, their effect against Japanese fighter and bomber formations on the missions over Darwin was much less, and losses were devastating.
In all, 38 Spitfires out of approximately 100 were lost to various causes, but combat victories, apart from Japanese aircraft lost to other causes such as lack of fuel, were only about a dozen.

- Only 3 Mitsubishi Zeros shot down by Spitfires in exchange for approximately 21 Spitfires.

Nakajima Ki-43s also achieved a 2-1 result in a single mission using Army aircraft.
Another career was that of the American Spitfires: first there were the Eagle Squadrons, which had employed American volunteers even before the entry into the war: first with the Hurricanes, then with the Spitfire Mk.IIs, for a total of 4 squadrons.

The Spitfire later became part of the 4th Fighter Group of the 8th AF. The aircraft were Mk.Vs, but in September 1942 the powerful Mk. IXs also arrived for No.133.

- However, it made its debut over France and in a single mission lost 12 aircraft against the deadly and experienced FW-190s.

The Spitfire was a high-performance fighter, although the Americans did not like its poor range compared to the P-40.
In any case, the career of the Americans of these units was very troubled: first came the P-47s for some units such as the 133rd; the 31st FG with its three squadrons obtained the Mk.V.
Some reconnaissance units had a continuous flurry of Spitfires, F-6s (P-51s), F-5As (P-38Gs), the latter however having great difficulty above 9,150 meters, so much so that in 1943 they were replaced by the Mk.Vs and then by the more powerful Mk.IXs.

- The real leap forward in Spitfire operations was Operation Torch, with units of the 31st and 52nd FG, directed against the 12th AF.

In February 1944, three of their Spitfires made a mistake in landing on Italian territory, where they continued to operate, and were captured, but not returned to service, by the ANR (Aeronautica Nazionale Repubblicana), while the pilots were helped to escape by the partisans.

- The 31st FG claimed 192 air victories and the 52nd another 164, considering only the Spitfire era and not considering the usefulness of these aircraft as tactical and strategic reconnaissance aircraft.

Thus, many of the Spitfires (6 squadrons) operating from late 1942 in the Mediterranean were actually USAAF, a fact which remained obscure until very recently.
The results must also be compared with the numbers, which were not particularly exuberant overall: 157 Mk.VB and C, a single Mk.VII, 9 Mk.VIII, 9 Mk.IX, as many PR Mk.IX and a single Mk.XII, plus the USN which had 12 Seafire I, 49 II, a Mk.XV and a Mk.47.

But these numbers seem largely insufficient for this operational career: there is also talk of 600 aircraft, and of as many as 274 Mk.V for the 12th AF alone.
It is known that the Mk.IXs of these aircraft, perhaps many more than those officially counted, especially if the 12 shot down in a single mission over France were really Mk.IXs, were not tropicalized (fortunately at the time Aboukir filters were in use, which were much less penalizing), while the older Mk.Vs, on the contrary, despite the large Vockes, were fully tropicalized aircraft and therefore, more reliable and efficient.
That the USAAF operated up to perhaps 600 Spitfires and to boot, claimed over 300 aerial victories, has remained a remarkable fact yet one that has been swept under the carpet of history for decades, perhaps not coincidentally.

- As for the Seafires, they never had the safety and autonomy of specifically naval machines, but nevertheless obtained satisfactory results over time.

Apart from the Spitfire Mk.IX Idro, capable of 500 km/h above sea level and 600 km/h at altitude, the naval types were mainly:

- The Seafire I: 166 examples.
- The Seafire II: 372 examples.
- The Seafire III: 1,220 examples.

equipped with a modified Merlin 45 engine with a speed of 578 km/h.

The Spiteful, and its equivalent Seafang, had been a last-ditch attempt to revitalise the aircraft, which had become obsolete not so much due to its own shortcomings, but rather to the advent of jet fighters: few aircraft had been produced as prototypes, and even fewer for the Seafang.
The Spiteful was a sort of Spitfire with a teardrop canopy, all the upgrades, including the larger tail, and a laminar flow wing.
In practice, it was the Spitfire with technology similar to that of the Mustang.

- With this one she reached 780 km/h, with a no less impressive low-altitude speed (700 km/h), but it was not enough against the Meteors and Vampires.

Incidentally, the Spitfire's wing remained unsurpassed even by this new structure, in terms of the Mach number it could achieve, which even exceeded that of the first jets.
The wing of the Spiteful would later become the base for the Attacker, a jet aircraft of the British Navy, precisely the first to enter service with it (in 1950), but which, despite being agile at low altitude and economical, was less successful than the similar Hawker Sea Hawk, which marked the sensational comeback of the rival from Supermarine, which for years had remained in the shadows among obsolete Hurricanes and defective, if not dangerous, Tornados, Typhoons and even the first Tempests.
Supermarine would go on to sell the Attacker to Pakistan, then field the similarly configured Swift, which however lost out largely to the Hawker Hunter, and finally the mediocre Scimitar carrier-based fighter, a sort of enlarged and beefed-up Attacker but with a similar formula.
Hawker, on the other hand, merged with BAe and continued the success that Supermarine had begun to lose from 1945 onwards.

Griffon engines

With a power output of 1,700 hp, the first Griffon-engined Spitfires made their operational debut in early 1943: they were designated Mk.XII and had been developed from the experimental Mk.IV model, which had flown in late 1941.

- The main difference between the Griffon and the Merlin apart from the increase in displacement from 27.2 litres to 36 litres was that it turned the propeller in the opposite direction.

This forced Spitfire Griffon pilots to reverse the rudder action during take-off to compensate for the gyroscopic effect that caused the aircraft to turn sideways during taxiing.
At the slightest inattention the plane would abandon the linear trajectory and, in the best of cases, take off on a curved trajectory: there were therefore many accidents.

- Once airborne, however, the plane proved to be even faster than expected.

During a test with a captured FW 190 and the new Hawker Typhoon in June 1942, Supermarine test pilot Jeffrey Quill, flying Spitfire DP845, one of two Mk.IVs re-engined with the Griffon, easily left the other two fighters behind.
When fitted to the Mk.XII airframe, the Griffon produced 2,035 hp: this gave the new version of the Supermarine fighter extremely high performance at low altitude, around 330 mph (540 km/h) at sea level, which allowed it to take on the Focke-Wulf 190 at an advantage and even destroy V-1s.
Given the new engine, the size of the cylinder heads forced the modelling of two long bosses on the sides of the engine cover, while a third encapsulated the magnets.
Flight characteristics included an excellent rate of roll, superior longitudinal controllability to the Spitfire Mk.V, excellent high-speed dive behaviour and, more generally, superior handling to that of other Spitfires in production at the time.

- The only real concern was the rudder, which was very heavy.

The visibility, thanks to the lowered nose, was also better, both in combat and in ground attack actions, with tests carried out in 45° dives (even if in practice, the aircraft was used as an interceptor).
As for climb performance, the Spitfire Mk.XII was good though not excellent, capable, however, of competing with the Spitfire Mk.V at least within the first 3,000 meters, reached in about three minutes, but inferior to the Mk.IX, so much so that the operational ceiling was estimated to be about 9,000 meters (28,000 ft), although climb tests were carried out up to about 11,000 meters (37,000 ft), however with the prototype, which was equipped with wings with normal tips.
An improved engine, the Griffon IV, was also developed, which increased the climb by about 3 meters/second and saved about 30 seconds for the 3,000 meters.
Even so, the Spitfire Mk.IX regained its superiority just above 1,200 metres, albeit much less markedly.

- The Spitfire Mk.XII remained, therefore, a fast machine, up to about 640 km/h (397 mph), at about 5,400 meters (18,000 ft), but a specialist in low-altitude fighting.

Around 100 of these were built, clearly an interim measure pending the development of a new Spitfire Griffon which would be more versatile as a multi-role fighter.

- Supermarine attempted to overcome the shortcomings of the Mk.XII by fitting the Griffon to the fuselage of the Mk.VIII.

The result was the Mk.XIV, of which 957 were built, approximately 400 of them the Mk.XIVE fighter-reconnaissance model.
The Mk.XIV had excellent performance and was easier to fly than the Mk.XII.
One of the improvements was the adoption of a longer throttle lever which allowed the Griffon's blistering acceleration to be more progressively dosed.

A new five-bladed Rotol propeller then ensured better use of the new engine's exuberant power, while the squared wing tips reduced the stresses acting on the fuselage.
The major innovation introduced with the Mk.XIV was the RR Griffon 61 or 65.
These new engines returned to the two-stage supercharger, as was the case with the Merlin 61s, whereas previous versions had a single-stage, two-speed one.

- Thus, the Griffon 65 delivered up to 2,035 hp (1,520 kW) at an altitude of 2,100 meters and 1,820 hp again at 6,400 meters.

For comparison, the Griffon IIB had only 1,730 hp at 2,300 meters and 1,490 at 4,270 meters, which explains the drastic drop in performance at high altitudes.
As a result, the Mk.XIV became an all-altitude fighter, as it was faster and climbed better than the Mk.XII: to 6,100 metres in about 5 minutes versus 6.7, and to 9,150 meters in about 8.35 minutes versus 13.
The performance gap between the new Spitfire and the German fighters was seen as very high, except around 5,000 meters, where the Gustav was still competitive in speed and climb.
But elsewhere the advantage swung significantly to the Spitfire, which outpaced it by about 60 km/h at high altitude.
The FW 190 was also outperformed at all altitudes, although it held its own at medium-low altitudes.
Handling was also superior, except against the FW 190 and then only in the case of rolling; in turns the Spitfire Mk.XIV, despite being heavy, equalled the previous Mk.IX and surpassed all other Anglo-American fighters of the latest generation, including the Tempest and Mustang; in climbing it was the best of the fighters tested by the British, even slightly surpassing the Spitfire Mk.IX.

- The dive was good, but not yet entirely free of the drawbacks seen with previous Spitfires.

The Mk.XIV eventually entered service with 610 Squadron at County of Chester in the spring of 1944.

Its firepower was three times that of the Mk.I and its maximum speed was 724 km/h (450 mph) at 7,924 meters (26,000 ft) with a rate of climb of 1,395 meters (4,580 ft) per minute.
It did not see action so much against the Bf 109s and the Fw 190s, but rather, very effectively, against the V1 flying bombs, of which it destroyed at least 300.

- And it was again a Mk.XIV that became the first Allied aircraft to shoot down a Me.262 jet fighter.

On the evening of 14 February 1945, Flight Lieutenant FAO Gaze of RAF 610 Squadron, on patrol over Nijmegen, Holland, in a Mk.XIV, after failing to intercept an Arado 234 twin-engined reconnaissance jet, surprised three Me 262s at lower altitude.

"I couldn't see very well because we were flying into the sun ," Gaze recalled . *"But I fired from 350 yards and hit the starboard engine. The 262 pulled its nose up slowly and turned to starboard, while the other two disappeared into the clouds. I fired again and hit the engine and fuselage again. It rolled over, going into the clouds. I followed it and as I emerged from the clouds I saw a plane explode on the ground a mile ahead of me. I claimed this Me 262 as destroyed and my wingman confirmed the kill."*

On 13 March, again flying a Spitfire Mk.XIV, Flying Officer Howard C. Nicholson of RCAF 402 Squadron over Munchengladbach claimed another Me 262 shot down.
The later Mk.XIVs were fitted with bubble canopies which gave Spitfire pilots an unobstructed view all round for the first time, however, these models now bore less and less resemblance to the fighter Mitchell had envisaged.

RAF ace Johnnie Johnson said: *"The Mk.XIV was a beautiful machine but it was no longer a Spitfire."*

These latest Spitfire models, bombing installations in France, prepared the way for the Allied landings in Normandy on 6 June 1944.

On that day the RAF command used a total of 57 squadrons of Spitfires and 4 squadrons of Seafires on various tasks, from covering the first landing squadrons to patrolling cargoes arriving on the French coast from England.
Again, Spitfire Mk.IXBs of 222 Squadron were the first Allied aircraft to land for refueling in the previously occupied territories at St. Croix sur Mer.
On 17 July Spitfires of 602 Squadron had a chance to kill Field Marshal Rommel but the Desert Fox escaped with numerous head wounds.

- During the German retreat, Spitfires and Tempests pounded the routed divisions causing losses amounting to 8 infantry and 2 armoured divisions.

It was a lesson in the use of air superiority and RAF pilots could be forced to fly missions up to 6 times a day.
V1 launches were the next problem the Spitfires had to face: to do this, some Mk.IXs, Mk.XIIs and Mk.XIVs were adapted to have sufficient speed.
In this task they were supported by the fast Hawker Tempests.
Furthermore, they were employed against launch sites on the still occupied continent.

- The Luftwaffe's last gasp came in early 1945 with Operation Bodenplatte, when, relying on surprise, 800 variously assorted aircraft bombed and strafed Allied airfields causing the loss of 200 aircraft.

German losses, however, were higher and as many as 300 aircraft were destroyed, dealing the final blow to the Nazi air force.
The Germans suffered heavy losses from their own anti-aircraft fire, the Flak, which no one had warned of the raid.
The later versions of the Spitfire were powerful and heavy, with Griffon engines capable of over 2,000 hp and strengthened structures, and were now very different in every detail from the earlier machines.
Despite this, the wing remained large enough to allow good handling, although by now speed-based combat was becoming

the most important factor, as demonstrated by US fighters against older-generation lightweight Japanese aircraft.
The Spitfire was , however, a propeller-driven aircraft, and its potential was not infinite: the advent of jet propulsion forced all air forces to confront a new way of understanding flight and combat.

- The major difference was the greater speed that the powerful jet engines offered, but along with less reliable operation and much higher fuel consumption.

Nonetheless, the Gloster Meteors and De Havilland Vampires quickly became the fighters of the future for the RAF.
The Spitfire Mk.21s had a long and difficult development, and their post-war career was cut short, like so many other aircraft, both by the end of hostilities, which cut orders, and by the advent of jet aircraft.
The various devices that followed were not very successful and were produced in limited numbers.
With the Spitfire Mk.21, while the wing had previously remained substantially the same, although profoundly modified, to make the most of the power and give up some of the maneuverability, a new wing was developed, with a laminar profile, which resembled a cross between that of the Spitfire and that of the P-51 Mustang, square as it was, but not perfectly rectangular in plan.

- Subsequent models were the Spitfire MK.22 and Mk.24, with a bubble canopy from which the Seafire 45 and 47 were derived, perhaps the best carrier-based fighters together with the Hawker Seafury.

The Spiteful also had a different name from what was now only an ancestor; with the Griffon engines and the new wing it reached almost 800 km/h, by far the fastest European piston fighter, but despite this it was not successful and was produced in few examples, some of which after being fitted out were not even completed or tested, being subsequently demolished.
The naval version Seafang also suffered an identical fate.
Supermarine was heading towards a rapid and inexorable decline, while Hawker, which had been cornered by the limited

Hurricane, and then by the problematic Typhoon, ended up replacing it by creating the most successful post-war fighter, the Hunter, which among other things vaguely reproduced the elliptical planform of the wings but married with a swept-back wing.

Technical Features

The Rolls-Royce Griffon was a 60° V12 aircraft engine produced by the British company Rolls-Royce Limited during the 1940s, used on some aircraft during and after the Second World War.

The Griffon was derived from a development of the Rolls-Royce R, used by the English racing hydrofoils that took part in the Schneider Cup during the 1930s.

The idea of using the Griffon on the Supermarine Spitfire fighter aircraft came in 1939 to Joe Smith, who had taken over as chief designer at Supermarine after the death of its designer, Reginald Joseph Mitchell.

At that time, however, Rolls-Royce was busy developing the smaller, 27-litre Merlin: this engine had already provided superior performance to the initial versions of the Griffon.

As development of the engine continued it was decided to test it in the Spitfire.

- The first fighter to mount the Griffon was a single example of the Mk.IV version (serial DP845), which in turn was a Spitfire Mk.III with short wings.

The engine version used was the RG2SM with a single-stage, two-speed compressor: the test flight was carried out on 27 November 1941.

Rolls-Royce introduced the latest developments in supercharging from the Merlin to the Griffon: the latest versions of the Griffon were equipped with a three-speed, two-stage supercharger.

The first production variant of the Spitfire to be powered by the Griffon was the Mk.XII: in this case the engine was a Griffon version III or IV producing 1,758 hp (1294 kW).

The subsequent Mk.XIV version was fitted with the Griffon 65.

The Griffon 61 was mounted on the later versions of the fighter.

The PR.Mk.XIX photo-reconnaissance version, produced from 1944 onwards and also used after the end of the conflict, was also equipped with the Griffon engine in the 65 and 66 versions.

It is worth noting that it was an aircraft of this version that, in April 1954, made the last operational flight of the Spitfire in the RAF.
The Griffon 101, fitted with a three-speed supercharger, was also fitted to the sole Supermarine Spiteful (serial number RB518): the aircraft reached a speed of 795 km/h (494 mph).
The Griffon was used not only on the Spitfire but also on the four-engined maritime patrol aircraft Avro 696 Shackleton.

Below is the data relating to the Griffon 65:

- Type: 60° V-engine
- Number of cylinders: 12
- Power supply: triple-body vacuum carburetor with automatic carburetion system
- Displacement: 36.70 L (2,239.33 in^3)
- Bore: 152.4 mm (6 in)
- Stroke: 167.6 mm (6.6 in)
- Distribution: SOHC 4 valves per cylinder: exhaust valves with sodium insert
- Cooling: Pressurized liquid: 70% water and 30% ethylene glycol
- Compressor: two-stage, two-speed centrifugal
- Intercooler: water-air installed between the second stage and the engine
- Power:
    - 2,035 hp (1,520 kW) at 2,135 meters (7,000 ft)
    - 1,820 hp (1,360 kW) at 6,400 meters (21,000 ft)
- Specific power: 0.91 hp/in^3 (41.4 kW/L)
- Empty weight: 900 kg (1,980 lb)

After the War

After the end of the conflict, the Spitfire was still used for years by the RAF in the United Kingdom, although it was gradually relegated to non-front-line roles.
Three PR Mk.XIX reconnaissance aircraft were retained in service with the RAF's meteorological Temperature and Humidity Flight, making 4,000 flights before being replaced by twin-engined De Havilland Mosquitos in June 1957.
Outside Britain, Mitchell's fighter took part in many conflicts in (or between) countries struggling to free themselves from the yoke of an empire, be it British, Dutch or French.
None of these, except perhaps the Arab-Israeli war, gave the Spitfire much of a chance to make its mark, as it often involved strafing Communist guerrilla positions in the jungles of the Far East, and the Spitfire was not the ideal machine for such missions.

The Arab-Israeli War

The conflict between the nascent Jewish state and the Arab countries was the only one to see Spitfires from several opposing air forces clash, as well as the last conflict in which Supermarine fighters were shot down.
In one of the largest clashes, on 22 May 1948, Spitfires from no less than three air forces were involved.
On that day, five Royal Egyptian Air Force Mk.IXs mistakenly attacked RAF Ramat David, destroying several Mk.XVIIIs on the ground.
The 3 surviving Spitfires, one of which was flown by Geoff Cooper, took off and shot down four of the Mk.IXs.
Shortly afterwards, Cooper himself was shot down by American pilot Chalmers Goodlin who was flying an Israeli Mk.IX.
In the last air battle of the war, on 7 January 1949, 4 Israeli Air Force Mk.IXs, one of the pilots being Ezer Weizman, grandson of the first President of Israel and himself a future President of

the Jewish state , attacked 14 RAF Mk.XVIIIs and Hawker Tempest Mk.Vs.
The IAF claimed three Mk.XVIIIs shot down.

Malaya Crisis

The last Spitfires in the Far East saw action during the Malaya Crisis, now Malaysia, between 1948 and 1951.
After communist guerrillas killed three rubber tree farmers, the British declared a state of emergency and on 6 July 1948, rocket-armed Mk.XVIIIs from 81 Squadron attacked a camp of MCP (Malayan Communist Party) guerrillas.
21 October 1949 was the busiest day for RAF fighters: the Spitfires and Seafires of 800 Squadron flew 62 missions: it was here that the RAF Spitfires (the Mk.XVIIIs of 60 Squadron) carried out their last offensive sorties, on 1 January 1951.
The last one ever was flown by ace Wing Commander Wilfrid Duncan Smith.

- Perfectly restored, the Spitfire Duncan flew that day, TP280, still flies in the United States today.

The Indo-Pakistani Civil War

The Indian Air Force, which had used Supermarine fighters in action at the Battles of Bagdam and Shelatang during the Secession, when Muslim Pakistan decided in 1947 to secede into the (still undifferentiated) Indian subcontinent of what was to become the Indian Federation, decommissioned what remained of its fleet of 159 Spitfires, consisting largely of Mk.VIIIs, PR Mk.XIs and Mk.XIXs, in 1957.

- The Spitfire's fighting career was thus over.

Supermarine Seafire

The Supermarine Seafire was a low-wing carrier-based fighter aircraft produced by the British company Supermarine Aviation Works in the 1940s.
Named after a contraction of Sea Spitfire, it was a navalized version of the famous Spitfire, previously produced by the company and adapted to operate aboard the British Royal Navy's aircraft carriers during the Second World War.

- The first version to be delivered to the Royal Navy was the F.IB.

It was essentially a version of the Spitfire Mk.VB fitted with a hook for arresting on board aircraft carriers: however, it was soon realised that the airframe was too fragile to withstand the violent decelerations that the aircraft underwent on landing and the part of the fuselage near the landing gear doors was the one that suffered the most.

- To overcome these problems, metal reinforcements were fitted at the weakest points and the side members were also strengthened.

Further modifications and role-specific equipment were implemented on the II version, which instead used the Spitfire Mk.VC airframe.
Like its "brother" Spitfire, the Seafire also had too short a distance between the two wheels and this could cause problems during operations on the flight deck.
The modifications resulted in the center of gravity being moved aft, which reduced the aircraft's stability at low speeds.

- The pilots therefore had enormous difficulty controlling the aircraft during landing and preventing it from stalling; there were numerous accidents.

Furthermore, the Seafire also carried with it all the defects of the Spitfire, such as, for example, the short range which, while

not a determining factor for a land-based fighter, was of enormous importance for a carrier-based fighter.
Other shortcomings of the Spitfire were its poor armament and the difficulty pilots had in making emergency landings due to its weak airframe : furthermore, fitting it inside aircraft carriers was difficult since the wings could not be folded.
The complete adaptation of the Spitfire to a carrier-based fighter occurred with the Seafire F.III.
It was the development of the F.II, but now had folding wings.

A Seafire F.XVII (SX336) with its wings folded.

A low-altitude version, the LF.III, was also produced, powered by a 1,585 hp Merlin 55M engine.
The Seafire possessed superior low-altitude performance to the Japanese carrier-based A6M5 Zero, however, compared to its American counterparts the F6F Hellcat and F4U Corsair it was less armed and robust.
In later versions the Seafire was fitted with the new and more powerful Rolls-Royce Griffon engine which increased its performance.
The first Seafires saw action in Operation Torch during the Allied invasion of North Africa, but most of their engagements took place during the Far East campaigns, where they operated

with 887 and 894 Squadrons of the Fleet Air Arm aboard HMS Indefatigable, which joined the rest of the British fleet in the East in late 1944.
They were mainly used in the CAP (Combat Air Patrol) role, surveillance cruise.
The Seafire was chosen because it had the best high-altitude performance and a lower payload capacity than the other aircraft the Fleet Air Arm had in service, the Hellcat and Corsair.
In this role the Seafire was decisive in the fight against Japanese Kamikaze, especially during the battle off the island of Iwo Jima.

- August 15, 1945 was the most glorious day for the Seafires who shot down 8 enemy aircraft and lost only one.

During the Eastern campaign 887 Squadron claimed 12 aircraft shot down, while 894 Squadron claimed 10, with a further 2 achieved before departing for Norway.
The Seafire's most successful pilot was Second Lieutenant R. H. Reynolds DSC of 894 Squadron with 4.5 victories in 1944/45.
The Irish Air Corps also used Seafires in the post-war period, although it did not have an aircraft carrier: the fighters were based at Baldonnel and were used like normal Spitfires, with their wings clipped when they were put away in the hangars.

- An attempt to recycle a Merlin engine from a crashed Seafire was made in the 1950s by replacing the Bedford engine from a Churchill tank, but the experiment failed.

2,334 examples were produced.

Technical Features

Dimensions and weights

- Length: 9.21 meters
- Wingspan: 11.23 meters
- Height: 3.40 meters
- Wing area: 22.48 m^2
- Empty weight: 2,814 Kg
- Maximum take-off weight: 3,565 kg

Propulsion

- Engine: a Rolls-Royce Merlin 55M
- Power: 1,585 hp (1,182 kW)

Performance

- Maximum speed: 560 km/h (348 mph) at 1,830 meters (6,000 ft)
- Cruising speed: 351 km/h
- Rate of climb: to 1,525 meters in 1.9 minutes
- Range: 1,167 km with external tanks
- Ceiling: 7,315 meters (24,000 feet)

Armament

- Machine guns: 4 Browning M1919 7.62 mm caliber
- Guns: 2 Hispano-Suiza HS.404 20 mm caliber
- Bombs: One 227 kg (500 lb)
- Rockets: 4 x 27 kg (60 lb)

Versions

F.IB

Naval version of the Spitfire Mk.VB.
166 specimens.

F.IIC

Carrier catapult hardpoints and reinforced train: 4-blade propeller.
1,645 hp Merlin 32 engine, which gave the aircraft a maximum speed of 550 km/h (342 mph), a range of 740 km (460 mi) with a service ceiling of 11,430 meters (37,500 ft).
Together with its armament of two 20 mm cannon and four 7.7 mm machine guns, it could carry 227 kg (500 lb) of bombs.
372 specimens.

F.III

Developed from the Seafire Mk.IIC, it had manually folding wings, powered by a 1,585 hp (1,500 kW) Merlin 55M engine; its maximum speed was 566 km/h (352 mph), a range of 750 km (465 mi) with a service ceiling of 10,300 meters (33,800 ft).
Armament consisted of two 20 mm cannon and four 7.7 mm machine guns.
The bomb load was 227 kg (500 lb).
4-blade propeller.
The Seafire Mk.III played a role in Operation Overlord, more commonly known as D-Day, on 6 June 1944 and was involved in the invasion of southern France, Operation Dragoon, on 15 August 1944.
1,220 specimens.

F.VI

1,675 hp (1,380 kW) Griffon engine; asymmetric radiators from Spitfire Mk.XII.
390 specimens.

F.XVII

Produced from the Seafire XV, all examples have a teardrop canopy.
Powered by the 1,950 hp Rolls-Royce Griffon VI engine, the aircraft had a top speed of 600 km/h (373 mph), a range of 1,120 km (697 mi) and a service ceiling of 10,550 meters (34,600 ft).
Armament consisted of two 20 mm cannon, four 7.7 mm machine guns, and 227 kg bombs or rocket projectiles.
232 specimens.

F.45

New Spitfire Mk.21 airframe.
2,035 hp Rolls-Royce Griffon 61 engine with a top speed of 725 km/h, a range of 645 km and a service ceiling of 12,925 meters.
Armament consisted of four 20 mm guns with a bomb load of 227 kg.
As the Seafire Mk 45 would not equip front-line squadrons, it did not have the folding wings of earlier variants.
50 specimens.

F.46

Similar to the Spitfire Mk.22 with teardrop glass roof.
It was powered by the 2,300 hp Rolls-Royce Griffon 87 engine and had contra-rotating propellers.
Its maximum speed was 700 km/h, a range of 700 km with a service ceiling of 12,500 meters.
Armament consisted of four 20 mm cannon and 227 kg bombs or rocket shells.
24 specimens.

F.47

The Seafire 47 would have been the last variant and the first to feature electrically operated wing folding.
It first flew on April 25, 1946.
Powered by the 2,350 hp Rolls-Royce Griffon 87 engine, it had a top speed of 728 km/h (452 mph), a range of 650 km (405 mi) with a service ceiling of 13,140 meters (43,100 ft).
Armament consisted of four 20 mm guns with a total bomb load of 680 kg or rocket projectiles.
No. 804 Naval Air Squadron was the first to be equipped with the aircraft when it received 13 in January 1948.

.

Supermarine Spiteful

The Supermarine Spiteful was a fighter aircraft built by Supermarine during the Second World War to British Air Ministry specification F.1/43: the Spiteful was to be the successor to the Spitfire and would have been powered by the Rolls-Royce Griffon engine.

At the end of 1942, Supermarine engineers, analyzing the structure of the Spitfire, realized that, although it was very robust (it could withstand almost the speed of sound), there remained a limitation to the aircraft, which could not have improved in speed.

- To overcome this problem, it was decided to adopt a new wing profile, similar to that used on the North American P-51 Mustang, with the aim of improving its aerodynamics at high speeds.

A new wing was designed for the Spitfire with the following objectives:

- Increase as much as possible the critical speed at which the resistance increases, due to compressibility, becoming serious.
- Achieve a faster roll rate than any existing fighter.
- Reduce airfoil drag and thus improve performance.
- The wing area was then reduced from 242 sq ft (22.5 m^2) to 210 sq ft (20 m^2), while a chord-to-thickness ratio of 13% was used on the inboard wing where the equipment is stowed.
- Outboard the wing tapered to 8% thickness/chord at the tip.

At the same time, to facilitate large-scale production, it was decided to abandon the elliptical wing for a trapezoidal one, similar to that of the American Mustang fighter.

To make the landing gear more efficient during landing, it was decided to move it outwards and to reverse its opening direction: on the Spitfire the landing gear opened inwards; on the Spitfire, however, it was made to open outwards, since by increasing the overall width of the landing gear, the risk of lateral overturning was reduced.

- The new wing was first tested on 30 June 1944 by Jeffrey Quill, on a Spitfire Mk.XIV (NN660), to verify the differences in flight between the two wing types.

The Spitfire with modified wings had superior speed performance to the one with the elliptical wing, but it also had several disadvantages, for example, it stalled easily, which made it uncompetitive with the Spitfire with the original wing, designed by R. J. Mitchell.
In the meantime, however, it became possible to solve some of the problems that plagued the Spitfire: the pilot's forward visibility and stability were improved by adopting larger rudders.
This last feature became very important after the introduction of the Griffon engine on the English fighter, which was much more powerful than the Merlin, but which greatly increased its general instability.

- It should be added that in the later versions of the Spitfire a four-bladed propeller was used, and on the aircraft NN664 even a five-bladed one.

These modifications resulted in an aircraft significantly different from the original, which was called Spiteful: Victor had been suggested, but the proposal was not accepted.
The Spiteful's enlarged rudders were also fitted to the Mk.22 and Mk.24 versions of the Spitfire and the Mk.46 and Mk.47 versions of the Seafire.

- This type of tail is known as Spiteful Type.

Between 1943 and 1944 Joe Smith suggested designing a new aircraft that would use the Spitfire wing and the new jet engine being designed by Rolls-Royce (later called the Nene).
This proposal was accepted and specification E.10/44 was published by the Ministry of Air which was immediately named Jet Spiteful.

The prototype (TS409) flew on 27 July 1946.
The prototype was never ordered because it was substantially no better than its competitors: the Gloster Meteor and the de Havilland Vampire.
The project interested the navy which issued the specification E.1/45.

The fighter, renamed Attacker, had a quick and brilliant career in the ranks of the Fleet Air Arm and the Pakistan Air Force.

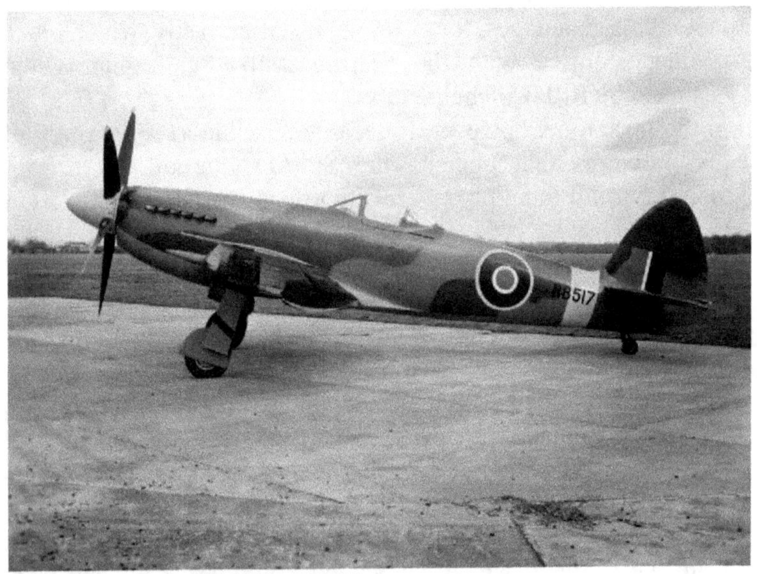

Supermarine Spiteful F.XIV, RB517.

The first version of the Spiteful was the Mk.XIV (the numbering followed that of the Spitfire from which it had been developed); 150 examples were ordered, but with the advent of jet fighters it was soon clear that the future would be marked by the new type of propulsion, and, so, only a handful of Spitefuls were produced.
However, as it was not yet thought that jet aircraft would enter service on aircraft carriers, a navalised version of the Spiteful was built - specification N.5/45 - which was later named Seafang.

- In total, 650 aircraft were ordered from Supermarine. The number of aircraft to be built was initially reduced by 260; a second cancellation left 80 aircraft to be built. The third and final cancellation reduced the size of the contract to 22 aircraft. Finally, of the original order of 650 Spitefuls, only 19 were built.

The Seafang featured folding wings, an arresting hook, was powered by a Griffon 89 or 90 engine fed by an oversized carburettor and used six-bladed contra-rotating propellers.
The first prototype was a converted Spiteful Mk.XV, but the success of the de Havilland Vampire design on HMS Ocean in 1945 made the case for a piston-engined aircraft obsolete.
After the end of the Second World War, Supermarine entered into a deal with the Société nationale de constructions aéronautiques du Nord (SNCAN) to produce the Spiteful under licence in France, but this came to nothing and the piston-engined fighters disappeared from the skies of Europe forever.

Technical Features

Dimensions and weights

- Length: 10.03 meters
- Wingspan: 10.67 meters
- Height: 4.09 meters
- Wing area: 19.50 m^2
- Empty weight: 3,331 Kg
- Maximum take-off weight: 4,523 kg

Propulsion

- Engine: One liquid-cooled Rolls-Royce Griffon 69 12-cylinder V-engine
- Power: 2,375 hp (1,772 kW)
- Propeller: 5-blade constant speed

Performance

- Maximum speed: 777 km/h at 6,400 meters
- Climb speed: 14.7 m/sec
- Autonomy: 908 km
- Tangency: 12,800 meters

Armament

- Guns: 4 x Hispano Mk.V 20 mm caliber with 156 shots each
- Rockets: 4 rockets of 140 kg each
- Bombs: two of 450 kg each

Versions

Spiteful F Mk.XIV

- 19 examples built
- Engine: Griffon 85 2,408 hp (1,771 kW)
- Weight: 4,510 kg
- Maximum speed: 767 km/h

Spiteful F Mk.XV

- 1 example built (later converted into the Seafang prototype)
- Engine: Griffon 89, 2,382 hp (1,752 kW)
- Weight: 4,620 kg
- Maximum speed: 778 km/h

Spiteful F Mk.XVI

- 2 built (converted from Mk.XIV)
- Engine: Griffon 101, 2,454 hp (1,805 kW)
- Weight: 4,510 kg
- Maximum speed: 795 km/h

Seafang F Mk.XXXI

- 8 examples built
- Engine: Griffon 61

Seafang F Mk.XXXII

- 2 examples built
- Engine: Griffon 89, 2,382 hp (1,752 kW)

Supermarine Seafang

The Supermarine Seafang was a carrier-based low-wing fighter aircraft developed by the British aircraft manufacturer Supermarine Aviation Works in the late 1940s for use by the Fleet Air Arm of the Royal Navy.
It was based on the Spiteful, which was a development of Supermarine's Griffon-engined Spitfire aircraft.

- At the time, the Spitfire was a 10-year-old project in a period of rapid technical development in aviation: the Seafang was being overtaken by jet aircraft and only 18 were built.

The Type383 Seafang was a development of the Supermarine Spitfire and the later Supermarine Spiteful to Air Ministry Specification No.5/45 and was essentially a Spiteful adapted for operations aboard Royal Navy aircraft carriers.

- It was equipped with an arresting hook, counter-rotating propellers to eliminate the torque that a single propeller would have caused on the aircraft.

It also had folding wings, a larger fuel tank and the Rolls-Royce Griffon 89 engine capable of 2,350 hp (1,755 kW).
Two models of these characteristics were built, VB893 and VB895, but there is no evidence that they flew before the end of hostilities: in fact, the Seafang flew for the first time in 1946.
It never entered production, but as many as 18 prototypes were built, some of which, however, never flew.
The Seafang F.32 underwent some trials aboard HMS Illustrious in May 1947 flown by Mike Lithgow.
Compared to its predecessor, the Seafire F.47, it did not show any noteworthy improvements: moreover, it could not threaten the performance of the new Gloster Meteor and de Havilland DH.100 Vampire in navalised version.
Added to this was the fact that her landing speed was no greater than that of the Hawker Sea Fury and the latter was chosen for the Fleet Air Arm.

One of two Supermarine Seafang F.32s.

During tests, the Seafang reached the incredible speed of 795 km/h and became the fastest piston-engined fighter ever built in Britain.
The Seafang's wing profile was adopted for the Supermarine Attacker jet fighter.

Versions

Seafang F.31

2,375 hp Griffon 61 engine and 5-blade Rotol constant speed propeller.
150 were ordered, but only 9 were built; the rest were cancelled.

Seafang F.32

Two prototypes were built, powered by a 2,350 hp (1,752 kW) Griffon 89 piston engine, folding wings, increased fuel capacity and twin 3-bladed contra-rotating propellers.

Technical Features

Dimensions and weights

- Length: 10.39 meters
- Wingspan: 10.67 meters
- Height: 3.82 meters
- Wing area: 19.50 m^2
- Empty weight: 3,636 kg
- Maximum take-off weight: 4,750 kg

Propulsion

- Engine: One liquid-cooled Rolls-Royce Griffon 89 12-cylinder V-engine
- Power: 2,350 hp (1,755 kW)

Performance

- Maximum speed: 765 km/h
- Climbing speed: 23.5 m/sec
- Autonomy: 633 km
- Tangency: 12,500 meters

Armament

- Guns: 4 x Hispano Mk.V 20 mm caliber
- Bombs: provision for 2 x 454 kg
- Rockets: provision for 4 x 27 kg

Supermarine Attacker

The Supermarine Attacker was a low-wing, single-engine fighter aircraft produced by the British company Supermarine Aviation Works from the late 1940s and used mainly by the Fleet Air Arm of the Royal Navy after the Second World War.
The development of the Attakker was due to specification E.10/44 issued requesting the supply of a jet fighter to the Royal Air Force.
In addition to Supermarine, the Gloster Aircraft Company also developed the Gloster E.1/44, an improved version of the Gloster Meteor, as a possible candidate, but the evaluation board rejected both designs in favour of the Meteor and the de Havilland DH.100 Vampire, the first RAF jet fighters to enter operational service.
Supermarine then proposed a navalised version of its design to the Admiralty, who agreed to evaluate its characteristics.
The Attacker prototype, Prototype 392, first flew on 27 July 1946, with test pilot Jeffrey Quill in command.
The Attacker's design was based on the straight, laminar-flow wings used by the Spiteful, a development of the more famous Spitfire, and intended to replace it as the piston-engined fighter, and for this reason the Attacker was originally nicknamed the Jet Spiteful.

- The aircraft was plagued by a number of design shortcomings that led to it being quickly superseded.

One was that it retained the now obsolete classic tricycle landing gear configuration, with the landing gear wheel placed under the tail which created problems during landing.
The complexity of redesigning a nose landing gear would have required a series of interventions, for example, on the wings to shift the loads needed to rebalance the aircraft.
Furthermore , such a configuration sent engine exhaust gases directly towards the ground, seriously damaging grass runways.

The first prototype of the navalized version was flown on 17 June 1947 under the command of Mike Lithgow, three years after the maiden flight of the Meteor.
The next supply order, confirming the acquisition of the model by the Fleet Air Arm (FAA), did not arrive until November 1949.

Supermarine Attacker F.1 'WA473 J-102' at the Fleet Air Arm Museum at Yeovilton Naval Air Station, Somerset.

The first production version, the F.1, was powered by a Rolls-Royce Nene Mk.101 turbojet of approximately 22.2 kN (2,313 kg) and was equipped with 4 Hispano 20 mm automatic cannons.
The F.1 version, which entered production in 1950, began to be delivered to departments in August 1951.

- The Attacker had a short career equipping the Royal Navy's Fleet Air Arm, not seeing any action during its front-line FAA service until 1954.

She remained in operational service with the Royal Naval Volunteer Reserve (RNVR) for a slightly longer period, before being finally withdrawn in 1956.

At home the Attacker was replaced by the more modern and capable Hawker Sea Hawk and de Havilland Sea Venom.
The Attakker was exported to only one foreign country, Pakistan.
Between 1952 and 1953, 30 examples were sold to equip the local air force, the Pakistani Fida'iyye, with which it remained in operational service until 1960.
The Supermarine Attacker spawned the Model-510, a swept-wing prototype that never saw a sequel, but which prefigured the Royal Air Force's "Supermarine Swift".
A total of 183 aircraft were built, including prototypes.

Versions

F.1: Naval fighter version as standard.

FB.1: Ground attack version.

FB.2: Strengthened version equipped with a more powerful Nene engine with 8 underwing pylons, capable of carrying 2 x 1,000 lb (450 kg) bombs or 8 unguided rockets.
24 ordered on 21 November 1950, 30 ordered on 16 February 1950 and a further 30 ordered on 7 September 1950, all 84 were built at South Marston.

Technical Features

Dimensions and weights

- Length: 11.43 meters
- Wingspan: 11.25 meters
- Height: 3.02 meters
- Wing area: 21.00 m^2
- Wing loading: 248 kg/m^2
- Empty weight: 3,826 Kg
- Maximum take-off weight: 5,539 kg

Propulsion

- Thrust: 22.2 kN (2,313 kg)

Performance

- Maximum speed: 950 km/h
- Climb rate: 32.3 m/sec
- Autonomy: 1,900 km
- Tangency: 13,716 meters

Armament

- Guns: 4 x Hispano Mk.V 20 mm caliber with 125 rounds per gun
- Bombs: 2 x 454 kg

www.ingramcontent.com/pod-product-compliance
Lightning Source LLC
LaVergne TN
LVHW010108170826
845678LV00012B/2291

* 9 7 8 2 3 7 2 9 7 5 3 1 5 *